All things being not quite so equal, people *STILL* want to do business with their friends.

HINT: To clim the ladder of success, you don't need more techniques and strategies, you need more friends.

Connecting is all about
your friendliness,
your ability to engage,
and your willingness
to give value first.

When you combine
those three attributes,
you will have uncovered
the secret of powerful
connections that lead
to **RICH** relationships.

Jeffrey Gitomer's

LITTLE
BLACK BOOK
of CONNECTIONS

6.5 ASSETS
for Networking Your Way to
***RICH* Relationships**

Bard Press
Austin

The Little Black Book of Connections

Published by Bard Press Austin, Texas www.bardpress.com

To order additional copies of this title, contact your local bookstore
or call 704.333.1112.
The author may be contacted at the following address:
BuyGitomer
310 Arlington Ave., Loft 329
Charlotte, NC 28203
Phone 704.333.1112, fax 704.333.1011
E-mail: salesman@gitomer.com
Web sites: www.gitomer.com, www.trainone.com

Cover Design by Josh Gitomer.
Photography by Mitchell Kearney.
Page design by Greg Russell.
Edited by Jessica McDougall and Rachel Russotto.

Printed in China by R.R. Donnelley.

Fourth Printing, July 2007

Library of Congress Cataloging-in-Publication Data

Gitomer, Jeffrey H.
  Jeffrey Gitomers little black book of connections: 6.5 assets for
networking your way to rich relationships
      p. cm.
  ISBN-13: 978-1-885167-66-8
  ISBN-10: 1-885167-66-0 (cloth)
    1. Success in business. 2. Interpersonal relations. I. Title: Little black
book of connections. II. Title.

  HF5386.G485 2006
  650.1--dc22
                                                              2006040243

Everyone wants to be rich.

Although most people
think being rich
is about having money,
rich is a description for
everything *but* money.

Rich relationships
lead to much more
than money.
They lead to success,
fulfillment, and wealth.

TURN THE PAGE!

The Myth of "The Little Black Book"

Everyone knows that a little black book contains powerful (and sometimes secret) contacts and connections.

When I was a kid, I always had a little black book that I kept addresses and (secret) phone numbers in. Everyone did. My mom, my dad, all my friends. In the '50s and the '60s, the world had yet to turn "designer." These days, it's hard to find a black book. Or if you do, it has a Ralph Lauren or Armani logo on it.

The myth of the little black book went anywhere from powerful business people and connections that you made, to names and phone numbers of girlfriends. But its purpose was and is universal: keep the names and the contact numbers of those people most important to you.

Today, the little black book has turned into a PDA or a laptop, or, pardon my expression, a "crackberry."

THINK ABOUT IT FOR A MOMENT:

How lost would you be if your
list of contacts vanished?
Let me give you the answer:
You'd go beyond lost and
into the realm of panic.

My bet is, if you're a parent and you lost your list of contacts, you probably couldn't even call your children, because all of their numbers are on some kind of speed dial, and no one remembers numbers anymore. Some of you never remembered them at all.

Personally, I can remember numbers from 40 years ago, but I can't remember numbers from yesterday.

In Atlantic City (1952), my phone number was 2-5740. The next year it expanded to AT2-5740. And I can remember every phone number through high school. But I have no idea what my daughters' phone numbers are, and I talk to them every day. That's not the power of connections, that's the paradox of connections. It shows you how delicate connections are. And it proves the importance of the most powerful words in the computer world: "back-up."

The question is:
Do you have a
little black book?

And if you do -- how powerful is it? Is it full of names of
people you hardly know? Or that hardly know you?

Today's black book is some kind of contact database:
Microsoft Outlook, ACT!, FileMaker Pro. Whatever it's called,
you have it on your desktop, laptop, PDA, or Blackberry.
And it's loaded with your important connections.

Take a moment and list your top ten most powerful
connections (the people who can make things happen, and
make things happen for you). Then ask yourself, "What have
I done for these people lately?" Or, maybe a better question
is, "Are these people you just call every once in a while to
suck their blood?"

People call me all the time and ask to buy me lunch so they
can "pick my brain." My response is, "I have a $500 per hour
brain-picking fee and I'll buy your lunch." That stops all the
blood-suckers, and I make about $5,000 a year eating lunch.

How many people
are willing to pay you
to go to lunch with them?

Back to your little black book.

In Harvey Mackay's incredible book *Dig Your Well Before You're Thirsty*, he asks the question, **"Who can you call at 2:00 a.m.?"**

It is without a doubt the most powerful question you can ask of your own network.

Who can you count on?
And who's counting on you?
Who would call you at two
in the morning? Is anybody home?

The science and sport of networking and connecting is not for the fast-buck, impatient entrepreneur or salesperson. If that's you, throw this book away, or *give it to someone who wants to build a fortune, not just make a sale.*

This **Little Black Book** is about connections and connecting, so that *your* little black book will become a success tool, not just a numbers database.

The Little Black Book of Connections is about:

- how you can climb the ladder without stepping (or crawling) on other people's backs.
- how to earn the respect of a powerful mentor without begging.
- how to build stronger relationships with customers, bosses, co-workers, vendors, friends, and family.
- the power of being in the same room with powerful people.
- how to connect with powerful people, and how not to connect with powerful people.
- how to say the right things to the right people in the right circumstances to make the right impression.
- how to maximize your connections so that they benefit from you -- and more important, how you benefit from them.

But the secret is to get them to benefit FIRST.

This book is dedicated to connections and connecting

It's always a thrill to meet a person who has some power or celebrity status. A famous business person, an author, a TV star, a ball player, a CEO of a big company, or to bring it down to the real world, someone who can help you get ahead. And oftentimes, you would rather meet someone who can help you get ahead, than meet the president of the United States.

As you move along in your daily life and seek higher achievement and greater success, you don't have to do it alone. Others can help you. Some of them actually want to help you and will take pleasure in helping you, as long as they feel you are both worthy and trustworthy. In other words, deserving.

Think about your most powerful connections right now. Make a list of four or five of them. (Hopefully, you have that many.) Next to each of their names, write a sentence or two about how they have helped you, and how you would like them to continue to help you. Under that, write a sentence or two about how you have helped them.

AHA! There's probably nothing to write about how you helped them. Or at least not enough.

Now make a list of four or five people that you would love to meet because they could help your personal growth.

It may be the CEO of a company, or someone who is the best in your industry. It does not have to be a hero, and it should not be a celebrity. Just four or five people who could help you take one step up the ladder of success.

Most of the time, these people are accessible -- if they believe that there's value in allowing you to access them.

I have very low-level celebrity status. My book is in the bookstores. From time to time people will recognize me in an airport or on the street. But I get fifty e-mails a day from people trying to access me. Time does not always permit me the luxury of accessing them. I have a team of people who help me respond. No, they don't respond for me. I respond myself. But they help me by doing the administrative part of responding, and taking my dictated answer. Do I get to 100% of them? No, but I wish I could.

I'll spend more time on those that offer value to me, or who want to contribute something for the benefit of all. Some of the e-mails are phenomenal. People give ideas that I get to share with other readers.

People who simply want to ask me a complex question having to do with their personal situation, or their sales life, will get a warm, friendly response from me offering answers at a rate of $250 per fifteen minutes. This separates the value givers from the moochers and looters (see *Atlas Shrugged* by Ayn Rand).

When I started writing, it was never for the purpose of having other people contact me. It was simply to help them. They contacted me because they connected with me. They identified with me through my writing. The connection was not physical at first. It was mental. And from the mental, they sought the physical.

Is anyone trying to make contact with you? If not, don't look at it as success or failure. Look at it as a report card for where you are at this moment.

HERE'S THE RULE OF "THE MORE THE MORE":

The more people are attracted to you, the *more* solid connections you'll make.

If people are not trying to connect with you, but you are trying to connect with them, that's also a report card.

The obvious object of the game is to *have them call you*. Until that occurs, or until you make a game plan for that to occur, you have to connect with them. And here's the great news: in the book, you will learn how to do both. How to make contact and how to create the law of attraction, so that others want to make contact with you.

Table of Contents

Expanded Table of Contents

ASSET 1 WHO DO I KNOW?

ASSET 2 WHAT DO I WANT?

ASSET 3 WHAT DO I DO?

ASSET 4 HOW DO I CONNECT?

ASSET 5 WHO KNOWS YOU?

ASSET 6 THE SECRET POWER OF CONNECTIONS

ASSET 6.5 THE VALUE OF CONNECTIONS

EPILOGUE CONNECTION MASTERY

The 4 connection questions that unlock the answers to growth and success!

- *Who do you know?*

- *How well are you connected?*

- *Do you know how to make a connection?*

- *Who knows you?*

"Who do you know?"

Think about the connections that you've made all through your life. Thousands of people. A small portion of them are still in your immediate life, your "today" life. Most of them have faded away for one reason or another.

Old friends from places you used to live or work, family members you really don't like, friends from schools, people you met in business who you no longer interact with, and casual acquaintances along the way. But all of them, in one way or another, had some kind of influence on you, either good or bad, and at one time may have even impacted your success or happiness.

It's important to reflect on who you know, because it encompasses who you have known. You don't actually stop knowing them. You just become disconnected from them. And probably a bigger question would be: ***Who would you like to know, but at the present time do not?***

Who you know encompasses who you can presently connect with easily and obviously. The better you know them, the easier it is to make a connection. How well you know them determines how early or how late you can call them on the phone.

**There is power in who you know.
Not just connection power.
Growth power. Success power.
Even fulfillment power.**

As you progress through these pages, you will understand the importance of not only knowing your connections, but keeping in contact with them, staying in front of them, and providing value to them. This will help you build your wealth of connections and your personal wealth from connecting.

QUICK QUIZ: If I challenge you to list your top ten most powerful connections, and your top ten most personal connections, could you write phone numbers next to the names from memory? I'll bet any amount of money you could not. I would bet even more money that it's more likely you remember their e-mail addresses than their phone numbers. In today's world of connections, a cell phone number and an e-mail address are more powerful than a business phone number and a street address.

I'VE BEEN NETWORKING WITH SOMEONE I KNEW AS A KID.
MY IMAGINARY FRIEND GOT ME AN IMAGINARY INTERVIEW
AT AN IMAGINARY COMPANY.

"How well are you connected?"

Everyone has a circle of influence. It may be a group of friends, it may be your coworkers, it may be your employees, it may be a club or a group you belong to. It may be your family. It may be business associates and connections. It may be friends and neighbors in the community.

Everyone has a group of people to whom they are connected.

Within these circles of influence, you may be a leader, or just a participant. Either way, from time to time, you make your feelings known, you make your philosophies known, you make your ideas known, and you tell others of your escapades and experiences for one reason or another.

The quality of your relationships determines their fate.

Sometimes you outgrow them. Sometimes you just move on. Sometimes good things happen to keep them together. Sometimes bad things happen that make them grow apart. But while they are present, they play a powerful role in your life.

They are the people that you rely on for information and support. They are the people you rely on for ideas and strength. They are the people who encourage you. They may even be the people who pay you.

Whatever the connection, they are also the ones that you will go to when you need something, or need to get in contact with someone new. Or will you?

Many people try to do everything on their own. Either they feel uncomfortable using their connections, or they don't know them well enough to ask for the favor.
BIG MISTAKE!

Think about it this way: If you meet and know (or knew) thousands of people in your lifetime, so do your friends and connections in your circle of influence.

You've heard of the phenomenon called "six degrees of separation." With six phone calls you should be able to get to anybody. Sounds more like a TV game show than a business strategy. But as I've discovered over the years, it's more true than you realize. If you take a moment and think about one person you'd like to meet or connect with, you probably know someone, who knows someone, who knows someone, who can get them on the phone. That's only three degrees.

The object of having a circle of influence is not just to use it to climb the ladder; it's also to build relationships with those in your circle so that when you need to climb the ladder another step, they are more than willing to come to your aid. As you read these pages, you will learn how to stay connected with everyone, forever -- assuming they choose to stay connected with you.

ONE BUSINESS CARD FOR YOUR WALLET,
ONE FOR YOUR DESK,
ONE FOR YOUR CAR,
ONE FOR YOUR HOME OFFICE,
ONE FOR YOUR BLUE SUIT POCKET,
ONE FOR YOUR BROWN SUIT POCKET,
ONE FOR YOUR GRAY SUIT POCKET...

"Do you know how to make a connection?"

Besides your circle of influence (people who can readily make a connection for you), you must rely on yourself to make connections. Others can help you, but in the end, if they don't help you, if they can't help you, or if they're unwilling to help you, then you gotta help yourself.

Most salespeople are taught to use some form of cold calling to make a connection. Don't get me started, but in my opinion, it's the single worst way to make a true connection. It is the fastest way to make a temporary connection, but the odds of that connection lasting are one in a thousand. Or less.

It's the same in job hunting. Calling on ads in the paper will rarely land you the perfect job, because the best jobs never make the paper.

The better way is **networking**.

You can network anywhere -- from a business after hours event to a ball game. From the theatre to a civic organization. From a kid's birthday party to a rock concert. Someplace where other people like you, or people you want to meet, congregate. Someplace where you might make a significant connection, assuming that you are **aware** and **prepared**.

Not all connections are powerful, nor do they lead to sales or deals. They're just connections. You never know where they will lead. You never know what will happen as a result of one person telling another person that you connected.

Savvy and confident people begin a connection with casual conversation, engaging questions, and meaningful dialogue, so that they can get to know the other person.

The object of connecting, and making a connection, is to make a good one. And a friendly one. You might call it a solid connection. A connection where you left a favorable impression. One that someone else might talk about after your initial connection is over. Maybe they'll show your business card to someone else. Maybe they'll pass along a piece of information that you shared.

As you read these pages you will learn strategies and techniques: to connect and engage, to be memorable in a positive way, and (in the end) to create positive word of mouth advertising about you.

SECRET: You can connect in such a positive and impressionable way that you create reputation at the same time.

"Who knows you?"

This is the most powerful part of making a connection.
And also the hardest.

If you have put yourself out in the marketplace as a person
of value, others will want to connect with you. Not all of
them will be good. Not all of them will be valuable. Most of
them will *not* lead you to the Promised Land. But some will.

Your job is to expose yourself to the marketplace in a
valuable way, so that you create some law of attraction,
and some method by which others can connect with you,
so that this "most powerful element of connecting" can occur.

Most people have no concept of this strategy. That's what
makes it so powerful.

A high percentage of those exposed to this "who knows
you" strategy will never do the hard work that it takes for it
to become a reality, making the "who knows you" strategy
even more powerful.

The reason I'm qualified to tell you about it is that I have
employed it for the last fifteen years and I can tell you it has
been the fulcrum element of my success. I discovered it on
accident, and now I use it on purpose.

As you read these pages you will uncover strategies and
ideas to create your law of attraction and begin to profit
from the philosophy and universal truth: **"It's not who
you know, it's who knows you."**

UNIVERSAL TRUTH
OF CONNECTING

It's not who you know, it's who knows YOU!

-- Jeffrey Gitomer

The 17.5 Strategies, Guidelines, and Rules of Connecting

IMPORTANT NOTE: Like any other process, connecting has rules and strategies. You may know some of them, but odds are you don't know them all. Offered on the next pages are most of them. (Hey, I don't know them all either.) These strategies and rules are simplistic -- but they are not simple. As you read them and begin to understand them, they will help you make connections in a better, more powerful way. Oh, one other thing -- you have to implement them.

1. Be friendly first, and everything else falls into place.
Friendly breeds likability and trust. People do business with people they like and people they trust. The twin of friendly is smiley. People who smile are 100 times more attractive than people who don't. Smiling not only sets the tone for others, it's the reflection you give them about who you are and how you think. *How friendly are you? How easy is it for you to make friends?*

2. Project your self-image in a way that breeds confidence in others. Your handshake is an indicator of your self-image. So is your dress. Everything from your hair to your shoes is an indicator of who you are and what your style may be, or not be. Projected image creates first impressions. And even though first impressions are not always correct, they are the ones that stick in the mind of the other person until corrected. *What is the image that you have of yourself? What kind of image do you think you project? Is that image acceptable to those you seek to connect with?*

3. Your ability to look someone in the eye as you speak to them is a tell-tale sign of your own self-respect. Make eye contact. It's not only a display of confidence, it's a display of truth and a display of respect for the other person. *Do you find it easy to make eye contact? Do you find it a sign of weakness when others do not make eye contact with you?*

I READ SOMEPLACE THAT EYE CONTACT IS A VERY IMPORTANT BUSINESS SKILL.

4. Your consistent positive attitude will breed positive responses and positive results. Everyone knows it's important to have a positive attitude. Very few people understand how important a role it plays in the way you communicate and the way you are perceived by others. Without a positive attitude, your words become cynical and slanted. Without a positive attitude, your demeanor becomes borderline or unacceptable. Positive attitude needs to be there all the time, in the background, as fuel to run your engine of life without toxic emissions. *Do you expect to have a positive attitude if you are not doing something positive in the morning every day?*

5. No connection is made without some form of risk. Dare yourself, accept the dare, and take the risk to make the connection. My philosophy of "no risk, no nothing" is most evident in making connections. You can lower your risk tolerance and risk barrier by being prepared, having the self-confidence, and projecting the image to take a short walk out on a thick limb to make the next connection. *Have you ever taken a risk and succeeded? Didn't it seem like less of a risk after the event was over than before you were willing to take it? Ask yourself why you're avoiding the risk rather than simply making an excuse about it.*

6. "Ninety percent of success is showing up," is a quote made famous by Woody Allen. He almost had it right. **The principle is: Ninety percent of success is showing up *prepared*.** Preparation is the key to success. Luckily for you, most people are either underprepared or unprepared. There's no such thing as being overprepared. **CAUTION:** Preparation requires work. Homework. Before hours and after hours work. If you are looking to connect, preparation is not the best way. **Preparation is the only way.** *When you show up to a networking event, how prepared are you? When you go to some kind of connection meeting, either business or social, how prepared are you?*

7. The less you focus on your motive to meet, the more likely it is that your connection will be successful. Most people trying to connect have some sort of motive or need. That's OK, depending upon when you make the ask. In my opinion, it should be later than sooner. First seek friendship and acceptance. In other words, drop your agenda and focus on connecting, not extracting. *Is your focus short-term gain, or a long-term relationship?*

8. Take a genuine interest in other people before you ask them to take a genuine interest in you. If you're trying to connect with another person, it seems obvious you'd want to get to know them. Not just to qualify them, but to learn from them. The best way to find out about other people is to ask questions. *Do you have a list of questions prepared in advance that will bring you an understanding of who you're meeting with?*

9. The sooner you can find something in common with the other guy, the sooner all the barriers will disappear. The link is not the secret. Finding it is. Find common ground, and you'll always have something to talk about. Think about the closest friends and the closest connections you have made throughout your life. I'll guarantee you the foundation is filled with things you have in common. *Are you willing to devote the time that it takes to uncover things you may have in common with a prime connection?*

10. The higher up the ladder you go, the more cautious people will be of your advances. Everyone wants to make powerful connections. A bigger question is: Do the powerful people want to make a connection with you? That depends on value, engagement, and the interest that you generate. In general, people with wealth are in no hurry to make big decisions. Don't you be either. Build confidence and build trust by going slower than you think you should. *Are you trying for higher level connections? Are they responding in a favorable way?*

11. Your projected image will often determine your ability to make a real connection. It's not "class," it's "first class." And image leads to reputation. *How are people referring to you behind your back?*

12. People judge you by every action that you take. They keep mental bookmarks about the promises you make and how you fulfilled them. You MUST always give a first class performance. You can't just look first class, you gotta take first class action and do everything in a first class way. *Do you always do what you say you will do? Do people refer to you as first class?*

13. Provide value. In order to build a solid connection, there must be a value connection exchanged. One-sided connections are short lived. Value-based connections are built to last. *Do you always provide as much value as you expect to get?*

14. Transferring your message with EXCELLENT communication skills. Connecting is about engaging in a powerful way that requires your message be delivered in an actual way. *How good are you at making your message compelling enough to act on?*

15. Staying in touch is more important and more valuable than making the initial connection. I use a weekly e-zine, and so should you. A weekly tip or tidbit of useful information sent to every customer, every week. *Do you provide a value message to every customer, every week?*

16. Since you don't know what day a powerful connection will be made, you must be ready every day. It's NOT just a matter of 100 percent focus; it's also a matter of paying attention to your surroundings. *Do you make new connections every day?*

17. Your present reputation determines your future fate.
Whatever your reputation is today, determines the near-
future of your success. And reputation is a continuous
building process. *How would you define your present
reputation?*

**17.5 Be yourself. Talk real, act real, be real, and you will find
that others will do the same in return.** In the classic Dale
Carnegie book *How to Win Friends and Influence People*, the
underlying theme is, "Be yourself." *How real are you to
others? How real are you to yourself?*

There are several reasons for being yourself.

First, it's the most comfortable feeling you can give yourself.

Second, it's obvious when you project it. It shows that you're
relaxed with it, and confident with it.

Third, it's always repeatable. It allows you to be consistent
in all of your communications with all of your connections.

And finally, it's the best and most honest way to act. It creates
an atmosphere for open dialogue and honest communication.

I have provided you with the personal rules and guidelines
for your connection (and life) success. Now it's up to you to
implement and execute.

It's up to you to connect.

ASSET 1
WHO DO I KNOW?

Calculating the value of who you know

Think of all the people you have met during your lifetime. Thousands. You've spent your whole life connecting.

Now is the time to harness the power of your personal network so that you can profit from it, and expand it.

This is a book of actionable items -- not a lecture on the obvious. Speaking of the obvious, Sparky, if you have thousands of connections, how come you only have a handful of e-mail addresses?

The easiest way to compile a list of who you know is to create the list by group: friends, business friends, customers, coworkers, important people you may know casually, those on your Christmas card list, relatives, members from groups you belong to, and people you'd like to connect with.

Once you've gathered your list of groups, call everyone you can and get their e-mail addresses. Find out what their biggest needs are for this year, and begin to think of ways to communicate answers to those needs. The good news is: Groups tend to need the same thing. One message to many is the way to go. Keep asking for input and keep giving valuable information. Before you know it, your list will grow just by one reader referring another.

Start small. Get valuable. Build your list. Build wealth. It all fits. It all connects.

The Little Black Book Connection Self-Test

Circle the number that represents your present achievement level.

1 = poor   2 = average   3 = good   4 = very good   5 = the GREATEST

1. People like me.
   1   2   3   4   5

2. I am constantly meeting new people.
   1   2   3   4   5

3. When I meet new people, I engage them right away.
   1   2   3   4   5

4. I have a GREAT personal commercial to introduce myself.
   1   2   3   4   5

5. I help other people regularly.
   1   2   3   4   5

6. I look to make connections for others.
   1   2   3   4   5

7. I network at least ten hours a week.
   1   2   3   4   5

8. I have my own Web site and publish useful information there.
   1   2   3   4   5

9. I have my own e-zine that goes out to all my connections.
   1   2   3   4   5

10. I am published someplace on a regular basis.
   1   2   3   4   5

11. I give speeches at industry events.
1   2   3   4   5

12. I know the most powerful people in my community.
1   2   3   4   5

13. The most powerful people in my community know me.
1   2   3   4   5

14. I know the most powerful people in my industry.
1   2   3   4   5

15. The most powerful people in my industry know me.
1   2   3   4   5

15.5 People call me to help them make a connection.
1   2   3   4   5

Score the test:

80 = Perfect score!
You're fully connected.

70-79 = Great score! An indication that you're
on the move -- UP!

60-69 = You're in the BIG CLUB of people who
think they're "pretty good," but in
reality are just getting there. Make a
game plan to intensify your efforts.

50-59 = You don't know the right people in the
right places.

40-49 = You're being passed over by people
better connected than you.

30-39 = You need Altoids and a makeover.

How I learned to connect
How I made connections

When I started connecting, there was no book to read on the subject other than *How to Win Friends & Influence People* by the late great Dale Carnegie. I read it. I devoured it. I even took the Dale Carnegie course back in the '70s. But my primary teacher was "by fire." I learned by doing and talking.

Let me give you some examples of connections I have made. These are stories that describe methods I used -- that you can use the minute you read them.

When I wanted to connect with a book publisher, I went to the bookstore, looked inside the best-selling books, and read the acknowledgments of the author. It *always* included the name of the senior editor (AKA the decision maker) and I began to make connections from there.

One day, my book agent (my literary agent) made me go to lunch with another author named Richard Brodie. Richard is not only the author of several books, he's also the author of Microsoft Word 1.0. One of the most brilliant and likable people I have ever met. Had it not been for a third party introduction, we would have never connected.

When I was in my early twenties, I went to a rock concert in a movie theater. I turned to my (then) spouse and I said, "I can do this. This is simple. All you have to do is buy an act, rent a theater, and figure out the details. I won't have to sell the tickets. If I buy the right act, fans will clamor for them."

When I went to New York City and visited several talent agencies, I found that one of the touring groups was Electric Light Orchestra, who coincidentally was my favorite rock band of all time. When the band got off the plane to do my event, I didn't know whether to shake hands, or touch them. Jeff Lynne and the rest of the group immediately became my friends. It was a case of both making a connection and being able to connect with those whom you admire.

In 1976, my two partners and I had an imprinted sportswear company that was growing by leaps and bounds. We needed an investor and somehow were introduced to a guy named Earl Pertnoy. After several negotiations we agreed that Earl would buy-in at 25%, and we would all be equal partners. On the flight back from Miami to Orlando, one of my partners declared that he wanted 26%, so that he and anyone could make a majority. When we got home, I called Earl, told him what had happened, and advised him not to invest.

One month later, I sold my interest in the business to my two partners. But Earl and I remained friends. He has been my mentor for more than thirty years. FOOTNOTE: I have never approached Earl with any investment ideas or opportunities since that day. His mentorship and his wisdom are far too valuable for me to think of him in terms of money.

Glenn Turner is my sales hero, guru, and attitude champion all in one. In 1972, through his tapes, movies, and books, Glenn Turner taught me how to sell and the principles of achieving and maintaining a positive mental attitude.

Yes there were others (Napoleon Hill, Dale Carnegie, Earl Nightengale, Bill Gove, and J. Douglas Edwards to name a few), but none like Glenn. I had never met him -- only heard his tapes and watched his movies -- until April 1995, twenty-three years after I took his first lessons. What a rush.

When we met, I shared the closing line from one of his famous stories, and I did it with a hair-lip speech impediment, just like he would have done it. He smiled and hugged me. And we've been hugging ever since.

Connections are a result of a combination of factors:

One, being open to receive the connection.

Two, being in the right place at the right time.

Three, being prepared to make the connection if you happen to be there.

Four, using your existing connections to make new connections.

And **Four-point-five**, being able to connect back, or return the connection.

REPEATED SECRET: One connection will breed another if, in fact, you can help the person that you have connected with in some way. Help them and they will be inclined (if not compelled) to help you.

Your present asset base: Your human capital

As you are looking to connect, it's important that your connections be segmented into three categories:

1. Those I already have. Define who they are. Define what they have done for you. Define what you have done for them. Define how you intend to keep them.

2. Those I need to have next. Define who they are. Define what you want from them. Define what you can do to attract them. Define how you intend to connect with them.

3. Those I hope to have in the future. Define who they are. Define what you want from them. Define what you can do to attract them. Define how you intend to get in front of them. Define how you intend to connect with them.

It's most likely that you have some form of contact database at the moment. But what you DON'T have is: 1. a clear vision or definition of what these contacts mean to you or can do for you, and 2. a value-based game plan to connect and get what you want from them. There's a .5. One is what they mean to you, two is what they can do for you and 2.5 is what you can do for them. Guess which one is the most powerful, and guess which one is the least powerful.

RULE ONE OF "THE MORE THE MORE": The more you do for them, the more they will do for you. The more you do for them, the more you will mean to them, and the more importance you will have in their lives. And of course, vice-versa.

In my experience, I have found that I get more pleasure out of "doing for my connections" than I do from "them doing for me." So to complete your asset inventory, each contact must be fully defined with an emphasis placed on **what you can do for them**.

MAJOR CLUE: What you can do for them means nothing unless you take some action to follow through and do it. Here's my recommendation: Take your top ten contacts and put one action item next to each name with a game plan to complete it within thirty days. If you do ten things per month, you will have given value 120 times in the course of one year. That's enough to get karma headed in your direction with a stiff breeze behind it.

 CONNECTION EXERCISE: Make a present inventory of your top ten existing connections, the ones most valuable to you. They probably represent a large portion of your present human capital asset base.

Define who they are, what they mean to you. Define what they have done for you. Define how you are connecting with them each week (how you stay in front of them), then, define what you are doing for them, and how you give value to them. This is the defining "connection" piece.

RULE TWO OF "THE MORE THE MORE": The more you provide them with value, the more they are willing to provide value back to you, and the more willing they will be to take your call and meet with you.

1

UNIVERSAL TRUTH
OF CONNECTING

Your mother taught you everything you need to know about connecting before you were 10 years old:

Make friends, play nice, tell the truth, take a bath, do your homework.

-- *Jeffrey Gitomer*

"Billy, do your homework!"
Connection Homework

Can you hear the words of your mother ringing in your ears? She wasn't just telling you to do your schoolwork, she was helping you prepare the self-discipline for life's work.

Suppose I told you that tomorrow you had to connect with the five people on your wish list that would help advance your career or your life. How ready would you be to connect with them? I didn't say how eager, I said *how ready*. Most people try to make connections before they are prepared.

In sales, for example, the second most coveted prize (besides the sale) is a referral. If someone gives you a referral, your anxiousness to make the connection will often ruin the opportunity that the referral presents to you. You call them too soon, introduce yourself, reference your mutual friend, beg for an appointment, the referral responds, "Thanks, but I'm not interested." And the opportunity is gone.

If you would have used your brains (instead of your wallet) for thinking, you would have asked your friend to set up a three-way lunch or breakfast where you, your connection, and his connection could all sit down and meet in a safe environment. This way, you have your best opportunity to engage and make a connection at the same time you are with the person who can affirm that what you are saying is both true and valid. A much more compelling environment. One that will most likely breed a successful outcome.

The idiocy of connections is that most people try to make them on their own, when, in fact, someone else could not only make them for you, but could make them in a way that would almost guarantee a successful outcome.

How many times have you tried to make a connection and got turned down? I'm not just talking about business. This started in the fourth grade when you asked someone to come out and play with you, or you asked Mary to dance at your grade school social. Rejection is part of life. The crappy part.

I can remember in high school when there were two YMCA "clubs" for the boys: the Rebels and the Vikings. The Rebels were mostly jocks. The Vikings were mostly intellectuals. We each had our jackets. Mine was red with white sleeves, and had a big black "V" on it. I wore it with pride. And all the people in my group were my friends. One day, when we were juniors in high school, we were voting on the acceptance of a new member: my friend, Kenny Artis. All kinds of interesting discussions ensued. Kenny was not your regular kind of guy. Editor of the school paper, somewhat of a loner, extremely intelligent, with an offbeat sense of humor. In the early sixties, offbeat often meant weird.

They voted him down. I stood up and quit, asking everyone (in what was my first official speech, now that I think of it) who the hell they thought they were to vote down somebody just because they didn't like him or had some prejudice against him. I talked about Ken for three or four minutes: my experiences with him, and how I benefited from his friendship. I asked the group to reconsider. He was voted in unanimously. Ken and I were friends then, and we are friends now, forty-two years later.

CONNECTION EXERCISE: (Here's your connection homework.) Pick five people you want to connect with and, using your existing base of friends and connections, arrange a meeting or a phone call. This is an exercise, one of several to help you move in the direction of success by making connections. It's also a report card on how powerful, and how effective, your present connection base is. Or isn't.

The exercise should take about ten minutes per call. And, of course, the way you make the call will determine its outcome. You can't just make the call. You have to PREPARE to make the call. In sales it's called: pre-call preparation. In high school it was called: homework.

If you have to make a connection, the best, and most powerful, way is to connect through others. I have given you the philosophy: *It's not who you know, it's who knows you.* When they don't know you, the next most powerful philosophy is: *If you don't know them, figure out who does know them.* In-other-words: **Do your homework.**

I APOLOGIZE. I SEEM TO HAVE EATEN YOUR HOMEWORK.

ASSET 2
WHAT DO I WANT?

1. If you don't know what you want, you'll probably never get it

2. Ask yourself who you have connected with so far, and what it has meant to you

If you don't know what you want, you'll probably never get it

That truth seems pretty simple on the surface, but think of the people you know that are undecided as to a career choice. They wallow. And most are miserable.

It's the same with people and connections. If you don't know who you want to connect with -- the right connections, or the best connections, will probably never happen.

Ask yourself these questions:

- **What do I want from networking?**

- **What am I trying to get out of investing my time in networking and making connections?**

- **Who am I trying to connect with?**

- **Do I need to dedicate more time to it?**

- **How many people do I want to meet a week?**

- **What have been my results so far?**

- **Who have I connected with, and what has it meant to me?**

Making connections
is a combination of knowing
what you want,
and **who you want it with.**
It's also a combination of
a focused game plan
and serendipity.

Sometimes it's the people that you make a goal to meet, and sometimes it's the people that you bump into or are introduced to. People you had no idea were potential assets until you met. But you were in the right place at the right time.

There's also the element of putting yourself in the limelight so that more opportunities can present themselves to you. If you're in a seminar room, you might be able to meet three or four people. If you're **giving** a seminar, you have the chance to meet all the people in the room. Or should I say, *all the people in the room will want to meet you.* (This is assuming you give a good seminar.)

Everyone has someone they wish they could meet. Maybe it's a business connection, maybe it's a personal connection, maybe it's a potential employer, maybe it's someone of the opposite sex, maybe it's a hero. If you know who it is that you'd like to meet, then all you have to do is figure out a way to meet them. Seems simple -- but it's not easy.

There are 2.5 basic ways to do this:

1. You can try to meet them on your own. Mail, e-mail, telephone, cold call, or "go where they go" and try to meet them. In my opinion, this is not the best way.

2. Get other people to help you with the introduction. Think of all the people you know who might be able to help you or who might know someone directly that can facilitate a meeting or at least an introduction.

EXAMPLE: One of my customers manufactures golf equipment. I'm looking to get my column in as many publications as possible. In our conversations, my customer told me he knows a guy at *Golf Magazine*. He asked if I would like a meeting to potentially get my column published. "Yes!" I screamed, and two days later, the *Golf Magazine* guy and I are talking about my golf column. It turns out he's not the editor; he's the national sales manager. Turns out he needs a salesman in New York City, and I know a phenomenal print-ad salesman in New York City who's looking for a better job. Now it's ME making the connection for my new connection. And, I have a meeting with the editor of *Golf Magazine* on my next trip to New York City.

That was an unplanned connection, but a powerful one because it was a third-party introduction, thereby giving me credibility before I ever had to say a word. The net result will be interconnection. Within an hour, he helped me, I helped him, and we became friends. Score! (Or should I say, hole-in-one!)

2.5 Get them to call you, or get them to know you, first.

For the last 15 years, the vast majority of my connections have come from people calling me first. Either by referral, or from people who read my column, people who read my books, or people who attend my seminars. While this is not a method that you can employ immediately, it is by far the most powerful method of connecting. I have already built credibility. People are calling me for some specific reason, and I get to decide yes or no -- rather than the other way around. Not only was my example serendipity, someone else, who called me first, arranged it.

SERENDIPITY PROVEN: I am writing this piece at 7:00 a.m. West Coast time, sitting in seat 3-D on my way from Los Angeles to Charlotte. As the plane is boarding, a guy walks by and interrupts, "I have seen you do a few seminars. You're fantastic!" he said. "And you're an excellent judge," I quipped. "I'd like to have you speak at one of our events," he continued. "Here's my card." Wow! A connection from out of the blue. That will most likely turn into green!

I KNOW SOMEONE THAT I THINK CAN MAKE ME A FORTUNE. ALL I HAVE TO DO IS MEET HIM.

WHAT'S IN IT FOR HIM?

JACK

Ask yourself who you have connected with so far, and what it has meant to you

Make a list of the ten most significant connections you have ever made. Do not include parents or immediate family members. Next to each name, note four things:

1. What you have in common.

2. What you have gained from this connection.

3. What you want to continue to gain from this connection.

And most important,

4. What you have given to earn and keep this connection.

It may help add
clarity to your
"What do I want?"
by clarifying
"What do I already have?"

Now make a list of the five people you would like to connect with. Next to each name, note four things:

1. **What you want from this connection.**

2. **What you may have in common.**

3. **How you intend to make the connection.**

And most important,

4. **What you have to give (your value) to earn this connection, and keep it.**

It's probably easy for you to list what you want from these people. But it's much harder to list what you will give to them, much less what you have in common.

HERE'S THE RUB: Once you know what you want, the easiest way to get it is to become a value provider. The easiest and surest way to "get" is to "give."

Providing value to someone is a whole new way of thinking. **It means give first rather than "ask for" first.** It means helping others so that they will look forward to helping you back.

Often when I do favors for people, or help them in some way, their immediate response is, "What can I do for you?" That question is kind of pathetic when you think about it. It is kind of a feeble attempt to say, "Thank you." And it's asking for information without having any.

Suppose I said to the other person, "Just make my mortgage payment this month." That would show them how silly their question was. I would rather have someone say to me, "I am going to go out and buy ten of your books and give them to my most influential connections." That would be phenomenal! And it would be in **action** format.

Most people don't think that way. Especially the ones that I have just done the favor for.

BUT HERE'S THE GOOD NEWS: I know I am going to get a random e-mail from someone who I don't know, whom I have never met, who has purchased and read my book that says, "I just read your book, and immediately went out and bought ten of them and am giving them away to my best customers." That would otherwise be known as "cosmic payback" or a "cosmic connection."

I have found that the more I give away, the more I get. But I almost never get it back from the person I gave it to. I can't explain why, it's just how the world works. If I could explain it, I would be in a much higher position than "writer."

Now let's get back to what YOU want.

You may want to climb the ladder.

You may want a better job.

You may want to change careers.

You may want some advice.

You may be looking for money for a project.

You may need an introduction to someone
at a higher level that you can get to on your own.

You may be trying to win a big sale,
and want someone who has
direct access to the big boss.

Whatever it is that you're seeking,
you have to define it
exactly to yourself,
or it will never sound clear
to the person you're
trying to connect with.

Once you define what you want for yourself, and you're
able to make some kind of connection with your intended,
it might be helpful to everyone (including you) if you're up
front about what you're trying to gain. Because if it's a new
person, someone you don't know, all they're going to be
thinking is, "What does this guy want out of me?"

If you call me, and you beat around the bush about the purpose of your call, I'm going to pin you down in two seconds by asking you the question, "How can I help you the most?" That question forces you to get to the point.

I think it's both funny and pathetic that most people, especially salespeople, think they have to beat around the bush in order to get what they want. **MAJOR CLUE:** If they were just forthright with a value proposition, they could win 80% of the time.

If the "value message" you offer me consists of, "Let me buy you lunch so I can pick your brain," think again. I have no time for you, and neither will anyone else. BUT if you just bought my book, and you want to stop by my office and have me sign it for you, and I happen to be there, and I happen to be free at the moment, you could probably get 10 minutes of my time.

The reality is, most of the people you're trying to meet don't have a book. But there are ways of connecting. In *The Little Red Book of Sales Answers*, I delineate a connection process called reverse CEO selling, in which you create a leadership newsletter and begin interviewing CEO's about their philosophy of leadership, publish a newsletter with their pictures, and send it to people of influence in your community or industry. If you want the rest of the details, buy *The Little Red Book of Sales Answers* from my Web site, www.gitomer.com, or visit your local bookseller.

What I have shown you so far is the tip of the iceberg. Sometimes figuring out exactly *what you want* can take years. It evolves. But if you want it bad enough, and you're persistent about it, even if you just chip a little away at a time, eventually you will get what you want.

HERE'S THE SECRET: Help others get what they want as you're seeking what you want.

I know that's a paraphrase of the old quote, "You can get what you want by helping others get what they want." It's a quote that twenty people have taken credit for. But the point is -- it's true. And in whatever form you choose to execute it, it will work for you in ways you could never imagine.

There's another old expression that says, "Good things come to those who wait." That expression implies that you're just sitting by the window waiting for the postman to bring you a winning lottery notification. Not hardly.

HERE'S THE TRUTH: Good things come to those who have patience, and take consistent, persistent actions toward what they want.

UNIVERSAL TRUTH
OF CONNECTING

2

Before you can GET what you want, you have to KNOW what you want, and make a GAME PLAN to get it.

-- Jeffrey Gitomer

ACTION PLAN: First create a "what I want" document.
A page or two about what you really want in life -- success,
fulfillment, and achievement. Then make a list of the people
you know who might potentially help you. Finally, make a
list of the people you want to meet that will help you get
what you want and who you already know that might help
you get to them.

After you figure out what you already have in your human
capital asset base, you have to make the rest happen
for yourself.

Now it's time to make a plan.
A game plan.
A plan of action.
Action that you MUST
take to make your "wants"
turn into your reality.

Your game plan must contain actions for meeting people
on your own and arranging third-party introductions. It
must also be a plan for getting others to call you. This takes
a lot more work. But it's worthwhile if you're willing to
make the effort.

ASSET 3
WHAT DO I DO?

THINK! before you act.
Then act!

Think of the people that you've known for ten or twenty years. Think of how valuable they are to your success in your career and your success in life. Now think about your trusted advisors. Take the thought deeper as to how you connected with them. If some of them are relatives, or even parents, that's a familial connection. But others are those whom you have met along the way -- that you have somehow associated with a point where your life would be less, maybe significantly less, without that connection.

3

Part of this asset is
how to make more connections.
But a bigger part is
you being able to tap into
your own resources,
and your own ability to
self-discover how
you made your
most powerful connections.
Then once you've done that,
I'll challenge you
to repeat the process.

The end result will benefit both of us. You'll make the connections that you want and the success that accompanies this process. And you'll refer this book to others. Maybe even take the online course that accompanies it, or purchase the iPod downloads, or simply send me a check thanking me (and don't be cheap about it).

3

**One of the most
interesting aspects
of connections is that
they may be priceless.
Your job is to add
as many gems as you can
by finding the mines,
digging the gemstones,
and then polishing them
to the point when
they become priceless.**

UNIVERSAL TRUTH
OF CONNECTING

3

The only difference between where you are right now, and where you'll be next year at this same time, are the people you meet and the books you read.

-- Charlie "Tremendous" Jones, author of Life Is Tremendous

"Houston, we have contact." Preparing to connect with aliens

For more than forty years, Charlie "Tremendous" Jones has espoused his legendary quote, "The only difference between where you are right now, and where you'll be next year at this same time, are the people you meet and the books you read."

Think about that for just a minute. And then think about what books you intend to read this year and what people are on your "must meet" list this year.

Want to make a bet? I'll bet you don't have either list. How about making the list right now?

Books I'm going to read:

1. _____

2. _____

3. _____

People I'd like to meet who can influence my career, or my life, that I am going to meet this year no matter what it takes:

1. _____

2. _____

3. _____

Now that that's out of the way, one small item remains: **doing it**.

In my experience, "doing it" is something that most people are "going to do as soon as they can get around to it, or find the time to do it." What a bunch of crap that is.

For any one of a number of stupid reasons, people (not you of course) preclude their own success by justifying their lack of action, or at least a delay in it. I often wonder if one of these people were having a heart attack, would they say, "I'll get to the hospital as soon as I can get around to it."

WHY SHOULD I DO IT TODAY, WHEN I CAN JUST AS EASILY DO IT TOMORROW?!

BECAUSE YOUR CAR PAYMENT IS PAST DUE TODAY, AND SCHEDULED TO BE REPOSSESSED TOMORROW.

Having the courage to connect

Within the next three years, I'll be writing a book called *Sales Balls*. (Clearly part of the answer for what's needed to make connections.) In order for you to become more successful, in order for you to achieve your goals and aspirations, in order for you to be able to fulfill your dreams, you have to be a person of action. Part of that action is your courage, your focus, your determination, and your ability to connect with others, and engage them in a way that they will want to connect back.

Most people who are afraid to connect, or are reluctant to connect, are that way for four reasons: they're unprepared, they have a fear of rejection, they have a limited self-image, or they have low self-esteem.

UNPREPARED is best described as the nervousness you feel when going in front of a group to give a talk, or going into a test where you haven't studied properly. The best way to overcome this flaw is to dedicate time and literally make appointments with yourself to prepare. Set aside more than enough time than you need, and try to picture yourself already in the circumstance. In other words, get ready for any eventuality within the framework of what you're attempting to do. For example, if it's a speech: don't just prepare and rehearse the talk, make a list of ten or fifteen questions that might be asked of you, and then prepare the answers for each of those questions.

FEAR OF REJECTION is a common feeling in everyone. Men are rejected earlier in life than women, predominantly because they get rejected by girls at a young age. Rejection in sales is the biggest reason for quitting. (Second biggest reason: poor management.) The best way to overcome the fear of rejection is to bask in the joy of acceptance, and mentally prepare yourself, thinking, "Each person that tells me 'No' gets me closer to 'Yes.'"

LIMITED SELF-IMAGE is "I don't see myself as worthy of meeting these people. I don't see myself as able to connect with them in a way that they would want to connect with me. I don't see myself as running in the same circles as the people I want to meet. I'm not a member of a country club, they are. I don't have my own jet, they do. I don't have celebrity status, they do."

3

HERE'S THE SECRET: Realize that all people are equal (pretty much equal). The image that you have of yourself is a mental one. You created it. Maybe it means you have to go out and invest in some image clothing. Maybe it means you have to hang around a better group of people. You didn't lose your image all at once. Neither will you gain it back all at once. It's a slow process that requires both mental and environmental changes. Once you begin to build your own image, your self-confidence will grow right along with it. An easy cure is to write a column or give a speech and picture what you will feel like after it's successfully published or delivered. Think how your image will change when people acknowledge you, congratulate you, and show their appreciation for you. It's a real kick in the ego.

LOW SELF-ESTEEM is "I don't think too much of myself. I may not even like myself." And this feeling comes about typically from environmental circumstances as you have matured. Someone telling you that you're stupid, or someone telling you that you're ugly -- and you being foolish enough to believe them. Parents, in an emotional moment, may have told you that "you'll never amount to anything" or in some way may have discouraged you from your dreams or goals of achievement. The best answer for this situation is to change your environment. Find supporters. Find cheerleaders. And find friends who love you for who you are, and who will encourage you to live your dreams.

Any of the above circumstances will require consistent hard work and dedication in order to overcome those temporary conditions that are not just blocking you from making connections, they're blocking you from succeeding. And the frustration that goes along with this cannot be measured. Don't take my word for it, just look at the number of Prozac prescriptions that are written in this country.

HERE'S THE GOOD NEWS: Courage is a self-inflicted quality that gains momentum every time you try it. Think about learning to swim. At first you're scared, then you jump in the pool, then you flail your arms, then eventually you begin to swim. And by the end of the day, or by the end of the week, you're diving off the diving board, head first into a pool of self-confidence. It's the same when you learn to ride a bike.

Transfer those lessons (learning to swim or ride a bike) into your world of making connections. And begin to build your own momentum by stroking and pedaling your way to the first one, and then the next, and then the next.

The part you have to get over

The biggest barrier in making connections is your mental state of fear fighting against determination. Fear will manifest itself in the form of procrastination. You'll put it off, and put it off, until you're hurting, and then you may take some action.

Think about your teeth and the dentist. Most people wait until they are in pain beyond what they can stand, and then finally cave in and get the tooth filled or pulled. It stems from fear. Not fear of the tooth, fear of the dentist. The good news is, when you're finished with the dentist, you feel great. Or at least relieved. And you kick yourself in the pants that you should have gone sooner. But your fear created the reluctance and the procrastination that could only be overcome when the pain was so great that you had to take some kind of action.

It's much harder to see that same analogy when making personal or business connections. The fear is still there, but because there's no pain associated with it, procrastination could go on indefinitely. And opportunities are lost.

The only way to get over the fear is to begin to develop self-confidence through preparation. And begin to develop determination by taking consistent small actions over time.

"Simple self-disciplines repeated over time will lead to success," is a potential life-changing quote by Jim Rohn.

My personal promise to you is that
once you have the determination to
make that first significant connection,
the second will be easier,
and the third will be a piece of cake.
A big piece of chocolate cake
with ice cream.

3

Once you have connected, you then have the challenge
to provide a reason or value for the other person to
stay connected with you. The longer you can keep the
connection, the more potential benefit you will each glean.

GLASBERGEN

WE'RE BURNING 20 CALORIES JUST BY SHAKING HANDS.
THIS RELATIONSHIP IS OFF TO A GREAT START!

Go slow. Become friends

"Billy, go out and make friends with Johnny," your mother said. Damn, mothers were smart. They understood the fundamentals of becoming connected. Make friends first.

As friendships blossom into relationships, report cards as to their strength and quality pop up from time-to-time. Especially when things go wrong.

> In sales and customer relations,
> the quality of your relationships
> will determine the outcome
> of events when there is a problem
> or issue with price, delivery,
> quality, or service.

I'm NOT saying that if you have a great relationship you can ignore important issues and skate by -- I *am* saying that a great relationship will act as a buffer and allow all problems and issues to be resolved harmoniously. And just to put the *power of the friendly relationship* issue to rest, it is also the single biggest factor in determining reorders.

The rules of business are not as tough as the rules of relationships. Relationships are hard to develop, take time to mature, and must be nurtured along the way. BUT once achieved, they are the most powerful force in the business world.

BIG PROOF: Look at the customers you WISH you had. The main reason you can't get them is that someone else has a better relationship with them than you do.

Here are the key words and thought-provoking realities that will lead you to rock solid RICH relationships:

GIVE VALUE: You strengthen relationships by giving value to them -- not facts about you. Get them leads or put them in front of contacts that might lead to business for them.

TELL TRUTHS: You build relationships by telling the truth even if it hurts or embarrasses you.

BEAT GOALS: Have an achievable plan. Win big. Develop self-confidence by winning bigger than you expected. Self-confidence is attractive. Customers are especially attracted to it.

KNOW KNOWLEDGE: Have as much knowledge about them as you do about your company and your product or service.

HAVE ANSWERS: Be a resource. Get to the point where they consider you a resource of information rather than a salesperson or just another acquaintance.

TELL STORIES: Stories help people relate. Tell them one, and they tend to tell you one back. Stories are personal. Stories are revealing. Stories are truth.

TELL HOW: Tell how you have done it with others. Tell how you will do it with them.

FIND LINKS: Part of the relationship building secret is to break the ice. Find something in common -- a link that ties you together. Nothing like growing up in the same town, having gone to the same college, or having worked for the same company. Gathering personal information let's you know where to start.

USE LINKS: Find stuff that helps them build their business, and surprise them with it.

GET PERSONAL: Use personal information in a creative, sincere way.

BE THERE: Stay in front of them without an agenda (asking for the sale). Just earn it with valuable information they can use.

BE FRIENDS: Perform acts of friendship as well as acts of business. Have fun. Do nonbusiness things with them.

Here are some bigger "clues"…

SECRET CLUE: Need additional information on any individual you're trying to link up with? Easy. Call their sales department -- they'll tell you everything.

RELATIVE CLUE: Want to know more about what makes a relationship succeed or fail? Look at home for all the answers. Your mom and dad, brothers and sisters, and spouse and kids have all the answers you'll ever need.

FRIENDSHIP CLUE: After you study your family relationship characteristics, study your friends – especially the way you communicate with them. Notice something different in the way you communicate with best friends as opposed to business people? It's relaxed, more truthful, and less manipulative – try that on your customers.

REALITY CLUE: How you treat others is determined by how you treat yourself. Are you treating yourself to the right preparation? Are you qualified to build a relationship? Do you possess the characteristics of giving first, professionalism, self-esteem, self-confidence, honesty, and integrity that are needed to make relationships work?

HERE'S THE REAL SECRET: If you think you "have it all together," think again. You must work on yourself as much as you work on those you seek to relate to. Looking for a way to evaluate your capabilities? The biggest judgment you make each day is the one in front of the bathroom mirror in the morning. Reflections don't lie.

Free Git✗Bit: Want a great checklist and self-test to check your personal improvement? If you're brave enough to take the test, it will reveal exactly where you are on the personal growth chart. Go to www.gitomer.com, register if you are a first time user, and enter the words LIFELONG LEARNING in the GitBit box.

The "How-To" of Networking: 6.5 Networking success fundamentals that work

Networking is simple.

Networking is powerful.

Networking makes connecting, and the connecting process, easier and more enjoyable.

3

Networking is *not* an optional before or after business hours activity. Networking is a vital and integral part of your success.

You *do* business between 9 and 5. You *build* business before and after "regular" business hours. The most powerful part of your business is not conducted during business hours.

How do you integrate networking into your business schedule? Ten hours a month of intelligent, selective networking can have a doubling effect on your business growth in just a few months.

Here is a list of 6.5 fundamental elements that will guide your networking to the moon.

1. Network smart or you won't get the right results. "I wish I could get more leads when I network." Or if you say, "I go to networking events, but I don't get many prospects," it means you're not following the fundamental rules, *or* you're not networking where your prime prospects might be. Or both.

2. Commit by marking your calendar. Our office has a yearly wall calendar with all networking events posted and a small bulletin board next to it to post the event promotional pieces or invitations. Personally, I try to follow the "50-butt rule." If there are more than 50 butts in one room, my butt is there too.

3. Event selection is as important as networking itself. Each week the *Business Journal* publishes a list of business events, and the chamber of commerce publishes a monthly calendar. Don't overlook social and cultural events as networking possibilities. Select those events that may attract your customer or people who you want to get to know.

4. Know how you can help. People don't care what you do, unless what you do helps them. Know what problems you can solve, not a bunch of boring stuff about what you do. Asking powerful questions and showing how you can help will gain the prospect's interest. Gaining interest leads to an appointment. The purpose of networking is to achieve engagement that leads to an appointment.

5. Practice by doing. Many people go to networking events; very few actually know how to network effectively. Practice the fundamentals and subtle secrets of networking by working a room. If you practice the rules you will have a better chance to succeed at it. All you have to do is prepare, show up, and interact.

6. Be aware of time. Don't spend too much of it with one person, or you defeat the purpose of networking. Your objective is to take advantage of the entire room. If you spend three minutes with a prospect, that gives you a possibility of twenty contacts per hour. Five minutes each = twelve contacts. Ten minutes each = six contacts. When you're in a room full of prospects, every minute counts.

The size of the event dictates the amount of time you should spend with each person. The larger the event, the shorter time per contact, and the less time you should spend with each person -- especially the people you know. To make the most of a networking event, spend 75 percent of your time with people you don't know.

6.5 These methods and rules have worked for me. You may not want to put them to use exactly as I do. Modify the techniques to suit your style and personality. Networking is a powerful, cost-effective, personal promotion and selling weapon. If utilized properly, it can provide the basis for your business growth.

If you question the value of networking, consider this…
If there are 100 people in a room, and you have two hours to network, you can speak to at least 50% of them and probably make thirty contacts. How long would it take you to make fifty sales calls and make thirty contacts in any other environment?

Don't slobber. The rule of drool. How to meet an important person

Most people make the fatal mistake of trying to push their way, or sell their way (or drool their way), to a connection. They say who they are, they say what they do, and then they beg for some sort of action or favor. It's no wonder they are afraid of doing it. It's a business form of begging. It's without substance. And it's prone to getting turned down.

Another fatal flaw is slobbering all over the other person with high praise and insincere compliments in order to work in your "beg."

HERE'S WHAT TO DO: Prepare yourself by doing research on the person you are trying to connect with. Find out what you could be doing to help them, honor them, or bring value to them. Also try to discover what you may have in common with them. Once you have that game plan firmly in place, then make the call. But that's not the secret.

HERE'S THE SECRET: Ask nothing for yourself. And be willing to walk away.

Think about it in terms of a salesperson trying to make a connection with a CEO. The salesperson has two options: make a sales connection or make a value connection. A sales connection consists of making a phone call, sending an e-mail, sending literature, trying to make an appointment, and trying to make a sale.

A value connection works in reverse. Fax over a sales lead to the attention of the CEO on Monday. Ask him to get it to one of his salespeople. Do the same thing Tuesday. Do the same thing Wednesday. Do the same thing Thursday. On Friday, instead of faxing the anticipated sales lead, call the CEO's administrative person and tell them you are the "sales lead guy" and that you wanted to give this next lead personally.

I will guarantee that not only will the CEO pick up the phone eager to take the lead, he will also ask what he can do for you in return. My recommendation is that you request either nothing or a 15-minute meeting. The opposite of drooling is value. Once you harness the power of that, you'll never drool again.

TRUST ME. PEOPLE LOVE DOGS. IF YOU CHANGE YOUR NAME TO FIDO, AND LICK THEIR FACES WHEN YOU MEET THEM, YOU'LL MAKE MORE IMPORTANT FRIENDS. BUT, WHATEVER YOU DO, *DON'T DROOL*.

How do I develop a powerful 30-second commercial?

What's the purpose of the personal commercial?
To engage a potential connection.

What's the objective of the personal commercial?
To engage a potential connection with information about them, that makes them interested in you.

Often referred to as an elevator speech, or a cocktail commercial, I named it a "30-second personal commercial" because I felt you would understand it based on all the personal commercials you've seen on television. Some of which grab your attention, most of which make you grab the remote.

The key to a 30-second commercial is the word "engagement." Can you engage the other person in a way that they will be interested in conversing with you? After the thirty seconds is up, you'll pretty much know whether they're engaged or not by the way they respond.

Once you deliver your message, your job is to begin questioning to find something that you have in common with the other person (hometown, college, kids, sports teams, computers). If you've engaged well with your personal commercial and you've found something in common, then it's likely you can gain an appointment, and potentially a customer.

Personally, I like to ask questions first and give my commercial second. I like to know about the other person before I tell them about me. But I'm *very* experienced at engaging.

IMPORTANT NOTE: No matter what type of commercial you give, make certain that the other person knows what you do when you're done. Being vague makes everyone think you're in some type of multi-level marketing scheme. Whatever it is that you tell people, be proud of it. And be enthusiastic about it.

What's the secret to a 30-second commercial? Keep it to thirty seconds.

Free Git✕Bit: Want some strategies and examples of personal commercial engagement? Go to www.gitomer.com, register if you are a first time user, and enter the word EXAMPLES into the GitBit box.

DO YOU HAVE THIRTY SECONDS SO I CAN GIVE YOU MY PERSONAL COMMERCIAL?

NO, BUT I HAVE FIVE SECONDS. CAN YOU GET RIGHT TO THE POINT?

The reverse personal commercial

You're at a big networking event. Hundreds of people, hundreds of prospects. You're armed with business cards, incredible product knowledge, and (if you must say so yourself) you're looking sharp. In short, you're ready.

You stroll and take a look at the rest of the networkers. Lots of food, festive atmosphere, a little to drink, and a huge opportunity.

BIG QUESTION: How will you take advantage of this networking opportunity?

BIGGER QUESTION: What strategy will you employ to engage your prospective customer so you can arrange a meeting outside of the networking event?

Your success depends on two things: your rapport building skills and your networking strategy.

Interestingly, rapport and strategy are strategically connected and intellectually aligned in a manner that you can employ, both at the same time, in order to make the most of each connection.

The easiest way for me to describe this is through my own expertise. I do sales training. I have several personal commercial options. I could introduce myself, "Hi, I'm Jeffrey Gitomer. My company trains salespeople at seminars and on the Internet. We're one of the greatest companies in the world." I could also mention the names of some of my big customers and offer to send the guy a brochure. That would be a stupid way of beginning a relationship, because I have no idea what the other person does, and I have no idea if he needs me.

So, let me give you the ultimate way to create fast engagement and phenomenal results…

I walk up to someone and by looking at their name badge I can tell if that person is a prospect for me. They're either a CEO, vice president of sales, or a sales manager. I begin my conversation with a brief exchange of names and by asking a direct question.

"Hi, my name's Jeffrey. How many of your salespeople didn't meet their sales goals last year?" This question immediately begins to qualify the prospect. This question immediately makes the prospect think, maybe a bit uncomfortably. This question immediately tells me I'm dealing with a decision maker. And this question is about them -- but they will respond in terms of me.

This person's answers will determine my direction. Remember, this is a strategy, not a pitch. Suppose the response is, "Seventy percent did not meet their goal." I would come back with one of the following responses: *Geez, that's horrible! What do you think caused that? Why do you think that happened? What kind of plan do you have in place this year to help them exceed their goals? Is there a monetary value attached to that achievement? Who is responsible for their success or failure? In your experience, what were the prime reasons they failed? Is it the people, or the market? What will you do next year that is different from this year? How are you supporting the team to encourage them to succeed?*

You see, I have twenty-five questions that I'm ready to ask based on the responses that I encounter (and I get them to give their commercial first).

Now the close. "Sounds like an interesting challenge, Mr. Jones. I don't know if we're a perfect fit or not. Let's have breakfast next week. I'll let you go into a little more detail and if I think I can help you, I'll tell you. And if I don't think I can help you, I'll tell you that, too. I'll even go so far as to recommend someone I think can help you the most. Is that fair enough?"

That entire engagement took less than two minutes. The other person did eighty percent of the talking, and I walk away with an appointment. Notice I never even said my last name as part of my sales pitch. I never said my company name. I never said how long I've been in business. I never said how great I am. I never listed my customers. What I did say was, "If I think I can help you, I'll tell you. And if I think I can't help you, I'll tell you that, too. Is that fair enough?"

For years I have written about the 30-second personal commercial, all about how to introduce yourself to a group or at a networking event. It's still valid, but I've modified it. This is basically an engagement conversation rather than a commercial. I've found over the years that people tend to skip the commercials so they can get back to their regularly scheduled program. The drama, if you will. And all I'm doing in my two minutes is engaging them in their drama and offering them an opportunity to analyze their problems -- so I can offer them a number of solutions.

ADAPT AND ADOPT: I've given you this networking engagement exercise in terms of me and my business. Now you have to adapt it to you and your business.

Once you've adapted your presentation mentally, you have to adopt the strategy as one you will use until you've mastered it. You see, this is not a simple networking strategy. This is a complex process that requires preparation and hard work.

Ask yourself this BEFORE you go to the next networking event: Do I have the right questions pre-prepared? Am I proficient enough to "engage" the people I meet?

Answer those questions "Yes!" and sales will double.

Free GitＸBit: **Want more examples of how to give a personal commercial?** Go to www.gitomer.com, register if you are a first time user, and enter the words REVERSE COMMERCIAL in the GitBit box.

Personal information leads to a relationship. And lots of sales

To establish the ultimate long-term relationship and to be memorable in the service you perform, you need to discover personal information about your prospect or customer. Information that provides insight. (And, oh yes, lots of sales.)

What do you know about what impacts your best customers and prospects? Ask any great salesperson their secret for success, and two things will be in their answer: a positive attitude and a computer full of personal information.

The famous "Mackay 66" brought attention to the importance of gathering personal information in the selling process. It's a form that asks sixty-six personal and business questions. But a closer look at this strategy reveals that information is only good if it's the right information. And that you use it to your advantage once you obtain it.

The difference between making a sale and building a relationship lies in your ability to get this information -- and uncover the other information it leads to.

The more information you have, the better (and easier) it is to establish rapport, follow up and have something to say, build the relationship, and gain enough comfort to make the sale.

3

How do you get all this information? You have to gather it subtly, slowly. A little at a time as the relationship grows. You can get this information from lots of places: secretaries, brochures, annual reports, and employees of the company (especially other salespeople). Take notes constantly.

If given a choice, people will connect with (and buy from) those they like and can relate to. If you have the information, and use it to be memorable, you have a decided advantage. Or you can decide "It's too much work, I can make the sale without it." This philosophy gives the advantage to someone else -- your competitor.

Free Git✗Bit: **Want to know the 40.5 Gitomer info-bits that you need to know about others to connect on a more personal level and build a relationship?** Go to www.gitomer.com, register if you are a first time user, and enter the words NEED TO KNOW in the GitBit box.

Networking not working? Try smart-working!

Networking is fun. It remains an enigma to me that more salespeople don't use it to replace the cold call (which ain't no fun).

If you network smart, it's the easiest way to make sales contacts. Hot sales contacts.

How to employ the science of networking is more of a challenge. The key is to keep it simple. First, figure out where you need to network to be most effective. (A major clue will be where your prospects or customers participate.)

OF COURSE I REMEMBER YOU. YOU'RE THE SALESMAN WITH THE FIRM HANDSHAKE THAT I MET AT THE NETWORKING EVENT LAST NIGHT.

Here are the essential questions to ask yourself for making networking an effective relationship and sales tool. NOTE: Your answers will determine your success:

• Do I have a 5-year networking plan?

• Do I have a list of the organizations where I can benefit the most?

• Who are the most important people that I must contact?

• How much time must I commit?

• Do I have my 30-second personal commercial written, recorded, and rehearsed?

• What are my expected results?

Here are some networking real-isms that will guide your success:

• **IT'S YOU.** To identify your best resource for networking success, just look in the mirror the next chance you get. (Pretty good looking, huh?)

• **GIVE FIRST.** To get what you want...you must give of yourself first -- without measuring.

• **DIG IN.** To benefit, you must commit to be involved, and then get involved. Become known as a person of performance.

• **BE CONSISTENT.** By attending meetings and events regularly, you will be seen and known as consistent.

• **SCORE.** People will do business with you once they get to know you and see you perform.

Here's the simplified 11.5 step version of how to win prospects and contacts at a networking event:

1. Target the people you want to meet.

2. Talk to them.

3. Get information from them that pertains to you.

4. Get them interested in what you do.

5. Categorize them on the back of their card as soon as you get it. (A. Wants my product. B. Knows someone who may want my product. C. Valuable contact. D. Professional contact. E. Social contact. F. Useless contact)

6. Qualify the contact. (If they're a candidate to buy, when are they likely to do so?)

7. Establish some rapport and find some common ground. (Make friends.)

8. Remember the information they've given you. (Write it on the back of their card as soon as you finish the conversation.)

9. Make the next appointment.

10. Write the commitment made on the back of your card -- the one that you give the prospect. Write the commitment on the back of the card he or she gave you.

11. Move on to the next person.

11.5 Follow up less than twenty-four hours after the event to confirm the commitment.

The paradox is that at a networking event everyone wants to sell. You may have to be a connector to help your prospect find connections (gather information) in order to have your best chance to be a seller. Networking success is dependent upon your ability to wear either hat.

UNIVERSAL TRUTH
OF CONNECTING

3

**Good things come
to those who have
patience and
take consistent,
persistent actions
toward what
they want.**

-- Jeffrey Gitomer

The key to getting what you want is TAKING ACTION (AKA DOING). I have given you clear instructions for identifying what you want, and I have detailed the necessary actions you must take to get what you want.

HERE'S THE KEY TO WINNING: Put action items into your daily work plan and dedicate the time to do them. Think of it as making appointments for your own success. Make at least three appointments with yourself a week. Make them one hour appointments, and keep them.

If you do this, you will have 150 hours of time dedicated to your success in one year.

NOTE: Make sure at least half of this time is spent one-on-one with connections that are imperative to your success. The rest of the time can be spent writing, preparing your e-zine, or taking other actions to be a value-provider.

A GOOD SALESMAN CARES ABOUT MEETING THE NEEDS OF HIS CUSTOMER. I NEED YOU TO GO AWAY.

Turning contacts into relationships

Two of the things I have found that
make the most impact on cultivating,
building, and enhancing relationships
are giving small personal things
or doing small personal favors.

3

Obviously, the key word there is personal. Over the past
year, I have developed the habit of giving my customers
autographed children's books for them to read to their kids
or grandkids (or keep for themselves).

*WANT TO KNOW THE BEST PLACE TO
GET AUTOGRAPHED CHILDREN'S
BOOKS? GO TO WWW.GITOMER.COM,
REGISTER IF YOU ARE A FIRST TIME
USER, AND ENTER THE WORDS*
BOOKS OF WONDER
IN THE GITBIT BOX.

I wish I could tell you the emotional impact that I have generated by giving these books. I cannot explain it. Nor can the recipient, who will often send me two-page thank you notes. These gifts typically cost me less than $20, but you cannot measure the value of "personal." Once you touch someone, your friendship with them deepens.

That's just one example of how relationships get built.

HERE'S THE SECRET: Touch something that is already a passion of the recipient. Instead of playing a round of golf, I have recommended going to a driving range at lunch, hitting a bucket of balls, and hiring a golf pro to come in and give your customer a personal lesson where they might shave a stroke or two off their score while you enjoy a catered lunch. For less than $100, you will create an incredible memory and make an incredible impression. And I can promise you the story will be retold one hundred times and you'll get phone calls requesting lunch dates that will amaze you.

Obviously you can strengthen relationships in business by doing more than you say you will do. For example, if you are selling equipment and you schedule a delivery and installation through another part of your company, make it your business to show up unannounced when the equipment is delivered and roll up your sleeves to help with the installation. This small gesture will win both respect and heart. Oh yeah, it will also win a sale and a reorder.

UNIVERSAL TRUTH
OF CONNECTING

3

Do what you say you're going to do -- what you say to others, and what you say to yourself. Offer value. Cultivate relationships. Do it even when you don't need anything in return.

-- *Jeffrey Gitomer*

ASSET 4
HOW DO I CONNECT?

1. Real-world connections. Real-world answers for how and why

2. How do I connect on...?

3. How do I connect at...?

4. How do I connect with...?

Real-world connections. Real-world answers for how and why

HOW DO I CONNECT ON A COLD CALL?

NOTE: There is no worse way to connect than this. Ever get a phone call from someone representing a police benevolent society or a fireman's association looking for a donation? It's a combination of insincerity, annoyance, and scam. You hang up. Even the legitimate unsolicited calls you get are at minimum an interruption.

Suppose you called from a telephone company, and your opening question was, "Mrs. Jones, I wonder if you know the three most underutilized features of a telephone." Using a strategy like this, you'll engage about fifty percent of the people. Which is about 9,000 percent greater than if you're trying to sell something. You can still get your sales message in, but the opening line has engaged them, rather than put them on guard -- or annoyed them.

HOW DO I CONNECT AT A NETWORKING EVENT?

A networking event should be looked at as a "business party." Most people there will be in a way better mood than they would be at their office.

The challenge with a low-level networking event, like a chamber of commerce event after hours, is that most people are there to sell something, and no one goes to that kind of event hoping they will find something to buy. It's one of the reasons that traditional networking doesn't work well. However, it's way better than cold calling. You're face to face with someone, and you can get to know them -- or should I say, connect with them.

If you're fortunate enough to meet a company owner or executive, your challenge is to be prepared enough to make a meaningful connection. This means being able to engage them about them, not simply telling them who you are and how great you are, and being able to connect by explaining how you help others.

If connecting is a game, then the strategy would be: *The slower you go, the more likely you are to win. The more you know about the other person, the more likely you are to win. The more prepared you are to talk intelligently, the more likely you are to win.* Notice I haven't said one thing about who you are or your product or services. Number one, it's a given, and number two, it's likely no one wants to hear about it.

Everyone goes
to a networking event
to better themselves
in some way or another.
Make sure you're prepared to
help someone else get better.

UNIVERSAL TRUTH
OF CONNECTING

The question you have to ask
yourself is: How can I make
people better as a result of
connecting with me?
Note well: This is not just
a strategy to connect at a
networking event, this is
a strategy to connect with
anyone, anywhere, at any time.

-- *Jeffrey Gitomer*

4

HOW DO I CONNECT AT A BUSINESS EVENT?

A business event differs from a networking event in that most of the people at the business event will have something to do with you or your business.

A group of accountants, a group of lawyers, a group of manufacturers, all getting together to exchange experiences and learn something new. Sometimes they will want to do business with one another, but most of the time not. Many times, they are actually competitors with one another.

The secret to connecting at these events is pretty obvious: know something about the business, or know something about the industry, that the average person does not know. And begin by sharing that in order to engage.

You might want to begin your exchange with a question rather than a statement. Have you heard about...? What do you know about…? How has … affected your business? When you ask for someone's wisdom, advice, or experience, you always have a greater chance of making a connection. Most people enjoy telling you what they know or what their opinion is. And as they're telling you their information, you can figure out how it applies to yours.

If you make the fatal mistake of talking before questioning, or talking instead of questioning, your chances for a solid connection are either diminished or lost.

Don't be fooled: Depending on what section of the country you are in, people may actually seem to be interested as you're blabbing. Don't confuse interested with polite. People will politely listen to you and then do their best to walk away. If you live in the Northeast, you don't have to worry about polite. People will just walk away. It's actually easier to make a connection in the Northeast because people will tell you where they stand immediately.

If you just follow the rules of connecting, by asking for their opinion or experience, you can connect anywhere in the world.

HOW DO I CONNECT AT A SOCIAL EVENT?

The key word here is, "social." Another phrase for social might be, "keep it light." Very few people come to a social event to do a business deal, or even to talk about business. And, depending on the social event, some people might even be a few beers south of sober.

The best thing to do is talk socially and try to make a friend, even though it might just be for the moment. Other people sitting at your table, other people standing in the same group, or someone that you're introduced to. If you're trying to make a connection, offer a business card. Most often, someone will offer one back, or, depending on their business status, may not have one with them.

In my experience I have found the highest-level people carry no cards. Offer yours, maybe put your cell phone number on your card to be certain they can connect with you, and let it go with that.

After the event, try to find someone who knows the person you want to connect with, who was also at the event, to help you. The host of the event will always know who attended and how to connect with them. That may be the best place to start.

One other personal note for you: If you're trying to connect at a social event, DON'T drink. Any connection you attempt while somewhat tipsy will leave the worst possible impression. If you're going to drink, maybe the best thing to do is carry your competition's card, and give them away.

HOW DO I CONNECT AT A SEMINAR?

If you're attending a seminar, most of the time a public seminar, where you or your company has paid for admission, your primary objective is to learn something new. However, all of the other people at the event are there to learn similar things, and because they're open to learning new things, they're also wide open to meeting new people, like-minded people.

I recommend that you attend every seminar you can, and try to meet at least a dozen people at each one.

<blockquote>
I have never gone
to a seminar,
and not met someone
of significance, or bumped
into someone that I knew
and strengthened
the relationship.
</blockquote>

Everyone in the room has the subject matter of the seminar and the seminar presenter in common. The intellectual exchange of information will be at its highest level for you and anyone you seek to connect with. You can almost go randomly around the audience and just start talking.

If you go to the seminar with someone you know, don't sit with them or talk with them the entire time. This way you will have the maximum opportunity to make new connections. It's also very easy to make appointments after the seminar with almost anyone in the room -- including the presenter if you're good enough.

As a presenter myself, people are often asking me if I need a ride to the airport, or need any other kind of assistance, so that they can make a connection with me. As the person on the receiving end of the connection, let me tell you that it works. I appreciate the ride or the lunch, and they appreciate the connection.

HOW DO I CONNECT ON THE GOLF COURSE?

You are trained to make the one hour sale in an office environment, but have no training to make a five hour sales call on the golf course. On the golf course everything is exposed. Your manners. Your ethics. Your knowledge of the game. And your personal habits. They'll never remember the score of the round, but they will always remember that you cheated on the third hole.

Whoever you present yourself as on the golf course -- is the image they have of you as the person they will be doing business with afterwards -- or not. The golf course is a great place to relax and connect. If you're too intense, the connection will be harder to make. Concentrate on your connection, not your game.

HOW DO I CONNECT AT A BAR?

Ever try to make a social connection at a bar and either not made the connection or just plain got rejected? The rejection does not mean you weren't qualified. The rejection does not mean you weren't attractive, or smart, or worthy. What it means is, your ability to communicate was somewhere between unacceptable and pathetic. Probably the best way to describe it would be a "bad pick-up line." It meant your communication skills were subpar in your ability to connect with and transfer your message to the other person in an acceptable way. I'm using this example because it's one that everyone has encountered either as a rejector or a rejectee. Your initial message must be compelling or attractive, or you will get rebuffed. (That's a nicer way of putting it.) The key at a bar is the same as the key in business: be friendly, be engaging, be humorous, be self-confident, and be yourself. Jerks get rejected.

HOW DO I CONNECT AT A RESTAURANT?

I enjoy casual conversation. Social conversation. When I go to a restaurant, I take a quick look around to see who else is there or who I might like to say hello to. If it's a good restaurant, there are always people waiting, and occasionally, you'll spot someone you know. If you know them well, any interruption is fine. They may be with people you don't know, thereby creating a new connection that already has an endorsement. I always give a card. I don't always get a card, but I always give one.

One night, I saw my American Express travel agent eating at the other end of the restaurant. I went over to say hello, and she introduced me to Mrs. Benny Parsons, wife of one of the original stock car drivers who's now a member of the NASCAR Hall of Fame. I told her I was a fan of her husband, and gave her a card and an autographed book. I told her that if Benny wanted to autograph an old photo, I would have no objection. Three days later, five gorgeous, vintage photographs arrived at my door.

Now some of you are saying, "Jeffrey, I don't have a book." Neither did I for my first forty-five years, and I still made tons of connections. Buy someone a bottle of wine or dessert. Send the waiter with a message. I have even paid for someone else's dinner without them knowing it until after I had left and the waiter gave them the news.

HOW DO I CONNECT AT A BALL GAME?

If you have invited someone to a sporting event, and are smart enough to be sitting next to them, you now have two or three hours to make a solid, personal connection. Both of you, or all of you, have the game in common. Start your conversation there. Talk "ball game."

I'm always interested in other games that my connection has attended. The other day I was talking to several business executives, and we were all recounting the first time our fathers ever took us to a ball game. I was amazed at the detail everyone could recall. It's remarkable how clear your memory is for something that happened forty or fifty years ago. You can remember where you sat, you can remember who played, and you can remember -- most of all -- being with your dad.

FYI: Mine was the Phildelphia Athletics versus the Boston
Red Sox in 1954 at Shibe Park -- later known as Connie
Mack Stadium. We sat on the third base side, lower deck. It
was a sunny day. The Athletics lost the game. But in the first
inning, the late, great Ted Williams stepped up to the plate
and hit the first pitch out of the park, over the wall in right
field -- just foul. On the next pitch, he hit it out of the park
-- fair -- home run! (I secretly cheered, even though he was
on the opposing team.) On that day, I became a baseball fan
for life, and I connected with my dad.

Think about the first time you went to a sporting event with
your mom or dad and how you connected that day. When
you recall those events with others, an emotional connection
is made and internally, you're smiling at the memory.

HOW DO I CONNECT WITH A COWORKER?

If you've ever read the book *Acres of Diamonds* by Russell
Conwell, then you know that some of the finest gemstones
are in your own backyard. If you haven't read the book, you
might want to do that next. In any business environment,
most people only know their coworkers superficially and
don't take the time to get to know them on an intellectual
basis, not just on a career or job basis. They also don't take
the time to find out what their spouses do, or who they are
connected with.

I recommend that you take fifteen minutes a day and get
to know someone at work a little bit better. If you find
something in common -- similar high school, hometown, or
childhood activity your depth of connection will immediately
go up 1,000 percent. If you only connect with one person a

week, next year you'll have fifty new connections, all of which are friendly, all of which you have something in common with, and all of which can potentially be helpful to you in time of need.

NOTE: All connections need not be utilized at once. If you have the right kind of database, you can earmark key people, key similarities, and key areas for potential help. Collect e-mail addresses so that you can connect or reconnect with anyone at anytime. Or maybe better stated, you can connect with everyone all the time.

I have several friends who utilize their close connection lists to see if anyone in the list knows someone they are about to go meet for the first time. That will only work about thirty percent of the time, but look at the leverage you create through the power of a third-party connection, either as an introduction source or a reference.

HOW DO I CONNECT WITH MY BANKER?

One of the most untapped resources in business-to-business connections is your personal banker. Banks not only have money (and lots of it), they also have customers like you. Thousands of them.

The key to connecting with your banker is to be proactive. Don't let your banker take you to lunch. You take them. Don't let your banker ask you for a financial statement. Send him or her one -- once a month. The more intimate your banker becomes with your business, the more likely they are to offer you ideas and try to connect you with others.

MAJOR CLUE: When your banker offers you a connection, you can rest assured it's a safe one. The bank already knows the financial condition of the person before they ever put them in touch with you. Keep in mind that banks don't take risks. Everything they do is measured.

Over the years, I have formed relationships with every banker I've ever had. My proactive communication allows me more financing than I could ever have imagined. And my banker provides me with a constant stream of people who can help me. So can yours.

HOW DO I CONNECT WITH INFLUENTIAL PEOPLE?

Connecting with influential people (big time businessmen, heads of organizations, celebrities, politicians, and other people of wealth or note) requires 2.5 things:

1. **An ability to get in front of them so they will come to know you as someone worthy of connecting with.** I do this through my weekly article, my e-zine, my books, and my public seminars. You better have a damn good game plan for getting to know them. Social and business events are one way, cultural events are another. The best is a third-party introduction. This will assure the influential person that you are safe.

2. **When you meet the person of influence for the first time, you better have something powerful to ask or something powerful to say, or you will have blown the opportunity from the very outset.** If you keep in mind the reality that people of influence probably don't need you, then you will realize that the key is to go slow and have something for them that they perceive as valuable. You don't have to give it to them right away. You can do it as a follow-up or, in some cases, wait until the next time you see them. In my experience, I have found that the slower you proceed with these people, the more likely you are to maintain some type of connection.

2.5 Have a way to communicate value after the meeting. More than a "Thanks, nice to meet you" note. Something that will engage them and make them want to see you again.

HOW DO I CONNECT WITH PROFESSIONAL PEOPLE?

Accountants, lawyers, architects, and other business professionals are all looking to grow their business. The top-flight professionals are already exceptionally connected.

The key to making successful professional connections is to start with your own. Your lawyer knows other lawyers. Your accountant knows other accountants. And they both know all of their clients and can potentially leverage your position with a third-party introduction.

Most business people fail to see the incredible potential of connecting with their professionals. Partly because they are already cringing at the bills they get every time they utilize their services.

DO THIS: Introduce an accountant to a lawyer or a banker. They LOVE to connect with one another.

I promise you that as you increase your friendships with your professional associates, as you increase your personal connection with them, the rewards will be incredible. Try to meet your lawyer for breakfast or your accountant for lunch, and pay the bill. And try to do it three or four times a year, as I have previously recommended with your banker.

PERSONAL NOTE: I have created an informal advisory group for my business consisting of my lawyer, my accountant, my banker, my financial planner, and the guardian of my 401(k). Every six months or so we sit down and talk about the present state of my business and the future plans for my business. This gives my professional team keen insight as to where I am now, and where I'm going. They will always offer additional assistance or additional connections to help me get there. I pay them for their time, gladly. And I respect their opinions. I do not always act on their suggestions, but I'm always mindful that they stand ready to serve and eager to help me succeed because I've been so open and honest with them every step of the way.

HOW DO I CONNECT WITH MY DOCTOR?

Nobody wants to die. But everyone gets symptoms of aging. When the symptoms become severe, the first person you think about is your doctor. He or she is the one who knows the state of your body, and the state of your physical well-being most intimately.

I'm fortunate to be a member of Signature Healthcare in Charlotte, North Carolina, a group of doctors who have formed a members-only practice where you get to spend leisure time talking with your physician. And I have access to the healing hands of Dr. Phil Arnone (the other Dr. Phil), my chiropractor and nutritionist.

These two medical connections have made an incredible difference in my life, because I am able to gain clarity on what is best for me physically so that I may maintain my highest mental state of alertness.

When something is painful to you, it dominates your thought processes and sometimes impairs your desire to move forward, as well as your creative juices. Interesting to me is that what I may perceive as something physically harmful to me, the doctor will diagnose as nothing at all. What this gives me is peace of mind and the ability to move forward, clearing my thoughts of what could have been wrong.

When you're feeling ill, it's not just a dominant feeling, it's *the* dominant thought process. It possesses you. And yes, you may have the mental fortitude to press forward, regardless of your illness or your pain, but never at one hundred percent. If pain or illness is your dominant thought, your ability to connect and achieve will be reduced significantly.

HOW DO I CONNECT DURING A SALES PRESENTATION?

Most salespeople make the fatal mistake of walking into a sales presentation and trying to sell something. Big mistake. No connection. The customer wants to buy, not be sold. If you follow my first rule of selling, "**People don't like to be sold, but they love to buy**," you will at once understand the dynamic of connecting in a sales presentation.

If you want to engage *them*, the presentation has to be about *them*, in terms of *them*, showing value and profit for *them*. If you are not successful in connecting in a sales presentation, your report card will be immediate. The buyer will ask for a bid or proposal, or give you an objection or stall.

The first sale that's made is the salesperson. If the customer does not buy you as a person, they're never going to buy what you're selling.

UNIVERSAL TRUTH
OF CONNECTING

The questions that you ask, the ideas you bring to the table, and your communication skills, combined with your passion, belief, and attitude, are the fundamentals of what it takes to connect.

-- Jeffrey Gitomer

4

HOW DO I CONNECT WITH A MENTOR?

Mentors are the guideposts on the road to success. Need help? Consider a mentor. Mentors play a major role in the life of a salesperson trying to succeed. Mentors give gold that you remember and can use to smooth the path (or find the path) to success. They provide inspiration and guidance when you need it most.

I owe more to my mentors than can be expressed in writing. They know it too -- I've told them. More important, I've shown them by adopting their wisdom and philosophies and putting their advice into action. Some of their self-evident truths were spoken to me twenty years ago and they're still fresh in my mind today. That's the impact a mentor can have on your direction.

4

I'M LOOKING FOR A MENTOR WHO CAN SHOW ME HOW TO GET RICH WITHOUT BORING ME WITH A LOT OF ADVICE.

SUCCESS CHALLENGE: Make a short list of people (possible mentors) you believe can impact your career. Find a way to get to know them. Find a way to get their success to have an impact on your success. I hope you do.

Free Git Bit: **Want to know the answers to 7.5 questions about how to find and keep mentors?**
Go to www.gitomer.com, register if you're a first time user, and enter the word MENTOR in the GitBit box.

HOW DO I CONNECT WITH FAMOUS PEOPLE?

Most the time connecting with someone famous (or infamous) happens by accident when you see them. Yesterday at the airport, when Jessica and I were going through security, she leaned over and said, "There's Mike Tyson." Sure enough, there he was. "I'm a big fan," I said to him. Immediately he extended his hand in friendship. I took it, looked him right in the eye and said, "I wish you every success." He thanked me and smiled. That was it. I didn't ask for his autograph, I made it short and sweet, and kept the memory. I think that's the best way to meet someone famous. Short and sweet. I don't think it is necessary to prolong the conversation, because typically, they don't want to talk to you for an extended period of time. There's no reason to.

I was boarding a plane (to who knows where) one day, taking my usual seat of 2C, and noticed that in 2A sat Hall of Fame quarterback Jim Kelly. "Hi, I'm a big fan," I said. "You probably don't remember me, but I attended your talk at a sales convention for a cellular phone company, and you autographed a football for me." He smiled. I continued,

"You probably don't remember that I was also a keynote presenter at that same convention. My subject of expertise is sales and customer service. You probably didn't get my autograph that day. So I've autographed my boarding pass for you." Handing it to him, I said, "I wouldn't mind you autographing yours and giving it to me." He smiled, autographed his boarding pass, and handed both back to me.

We had a good laugh, and talked football for about half the flight. My mind at the time immediately went to the book title, "You don't have to win the Super Bowl to be a champion," but not knowing his feelings, and not wanting to overstep my bounds, I never spoke it out loud. Three years later, I got a call from Tom, a connection I made in Charlotte, who had moved to Buffalo. He said that Hall of Fame quarterback Jim Kelly was looking to make some back-of-the-room products and Tom knew I had a studio. I met with some of Jim Kelly's people and came up with the idea for a book that we would co-write titled, *Be Your Own Quarterback: Six Points and an Extra Point or Two.*

Six months later, Jim Kelly and I spent two days together creating the foundation for the book and filming some of its content. We had another laugh about the boarding pass incident and now have formed a connection that has blossomed into a relationship. One that will be both profitable and personal. One that will be both meaningful to other people, and meaningful to us.

Connections with celebrities go very slow. Don't overstep your boundaries. Especially those that might intrude on the feelings of others. If something is meant to be, somehow it will happen.

HOW DO I CONNECT WITH MY CHILDREN?

Did you ever notice that every parent who finds out his kid is on drugs is surprised? Parents are usually the last ones to know about their children's actions. What a sad state of affairs. Connecting with your children is a reality-based thought combined with a reality-based process, so that you can create open and truthful communication with your kids. The key is to start early, start positive, stay enthusiastic, be helpful, and offer encouragement.

HOW DO I CONNECT DURING A CONVERSATION?

Everyone wants to talk about themselves. They love retelling their own stories about a success they just had or bragging about their kids, or their spouse, or their vacation, or their new car, or their new house. This type of conversation furthers a connection. But people seem to revel equally in talking about what's wrong: health, an accident, a layoff, something on their dark side. None of the negative furthers a connection.

I have found that by asking others their opinion, or getting their ideas or feedback, or finding out what their experience has been, I am able to connect much more deeply, and much more quickly, than if I talk about myself.

When I am engaged in a conversation with someone, I want to find out more about them: what they do, how they think, and what their philosophies are. These facts and opinions will help me discover if we have something in common (the link) that will get me connected in a way that I can begin a friendship or a relationship.

Not everyone is a connection, but each person you meet is an exercise in connecting.

If people ask me about me and what I do, I try to keep it brief, I try to inject humor, and I try not to "top" them. I believe my accomplishments are impressive enough without me having to drone on about them. If someone asks me about my books, for example, I may talk a little bit and then ask, "Have you ever thought about writing yourself?" or "Have you ever written anything that's been published?" If they have, now I have a link. Most people who have been published are frustrated and don't really know what to do about it or how to maximize the value of it.

Often I am able to offer help and ideas to aid them in their quest for greater exposure or market positioning. This deepens the link.

I'm not looking for someone to owe me something, rather I will collect another "cosmic thank you" and be comfortable with the feeling that someone in the universe will someday pay me back. This philosophy has worked for me for the past thirty years, and I intend to continue it indefinitely.

The famous Dale Carnegie quote says it best: "You can close more business in two months by becoming interested in other people than you can in two years by trying to get people interested in you."

HOW DO I CONNECT WITH WORDS?

In my customer service book, *Customer Satisfaction Is Worthless, Customer Loyalty Is Priceless*, I wrote a chapter about how your first words set the tone. Whatever you say first creates a mental image, a thought process, and the feeling of acceptance or rejection. It's part of what we have come to know as first impression. Just like your clothing, people form an instant impression from your words. If they can't see you (if you call them on the phone), then your words have even more impact.

Let me give you an example that you've all heard. Someone comes into the room to speak to the group. It's early in the morning. The speaker gets up to the microphone and the first thing that he or she says is, "Good morning!" The audience meekly replies, "Good morning." The speaker then responds, "I said, Good morning!" in a louder voice. Whereupon the audience screams back, "GOOD MORNING!" but is secretly giving the speaker the finger. The speaker has manipulated the audience against their will, has instantly become either unconnectable or less connectable, and will spend the next ten minutes trying to recover or establish him or herself. When you manipulate people against their will, they resent it.

If you're trying to connect on the phone (you don't know the other person) and you ask the fatal question, "How are you today?" you kill yourself before you start. You don't *really* care how they are, and all the other person wants to know is, "Who the hell are you, and what do you want?"

I recommend people start with a question rather than a statement. I further recommend that you don't even say your name. If someone is interested in who you are, they'll ask. Have you ever seen some meaningless announcer on television say their name before they start? Why do they have to say their name? Why don't they just wear a shirt with their name on it? (I do.) That way they don't have to say who they are. It's on there all the time. If you have to say your name, something's wrong. Can you imagine Frank Sinatra in a television interview starting out by saying, "Hi, I'm Frank Sinatra, and I'm a singer"?

Your name is the last thing people want to hear, and the last thing they'll remember. If you want someone to remember your name, don't say it, just give them your business card.

I have a hard time
remembering anyone's name,
because their name doesn't
mean anything to me until
I find out who they are,
and how they think.
I then try to discover
what they want,
and see if I can help.
Because, if I can help,
I can make a solid,
deep connection.

ASSET 5
WHO KNOWS YOU?

1. The first steps in getting known

2. Master the big 8.5 elements of positioning: The art of becoming known as a valued authority

3. What to do with those you attract

4. Getting in front of people who can say "Yes!" to you

5. What are the three secrets of getting known? (HINT: writing, e-zine, speaking)

6. A few more thoughts on getting known

The first steps in getting known

Becoming well known,
or at least well known
among your prospective
customers or connections,
is the single most
valuable element in the
entire connection process.

Tiger Woods doesn't make sales calls. People call him.
Oprah Winfrey doesn't make sales calls. People call her.
The better known you become, the more people will *want*
to connect with you. When you are an unknown, you have
to reach out to make the connection.

Obviously you can't go from being a relative nobody to
being a high profile celebrity overnight. The key is to start
with small actions.

The simple answer is to put yourself in front of people who
can say "Yes" to you. Or, put yourself in front of people that
you want to become known to. I have accomplished this by
writing and speaking. It can also be accomplished by joining
organizations, having your own blog, creating ideas, and
becoming better known as a person of value.

It's most interesting to me that every single company in the world tries to teach salespeople how to sell. Nothing could be more backwards or ineffective. What they should be teaching is *how to position, how to promote, how to provide value, how to communicate, how to make presentations, how to engage,* and *how to connect.* If you employ my first rule of selling, **People don't like to be sold, but they love to buy**, then you will understand that learning "how to sell" goes against the grain of human nature.

It's a hell of a lot easier to build trust by providing value than it is to make a sales pitch.

I've built a career by providing value. I've built wealth and success by providing value. It is not always directed value. Most of it is just value thrown out to the marketplace for acceptance. And those who accept will connect with me.

I do it with a weekly column, and I do it with a weekly e-mail magazine called *Sales Caffeine.* And so can you. But don't expect the response to be instant and overwhelming. As of this writing, I've been at it for fifteen years. That may seem like a long time to you, but I can promise you it's only been a heartbeat to me. It's a constant struggle, and at the same time a constant joy. But it's a slowly evolving process. One that requires patience, nuturing, consistency, and a dedication to excellence.

When I first moved to Charlotte, North Carolina (1988), I was flat broke. Under flat broke. I began to network. I began to speak. I began to consult. And eventually that led to writing (eventually is a four-year period of time). I was still relatively broke in 1992 when I began to write.

But, in 1990, I gave a talk to a singles group at the local
Methodist Church. The title of the talk was "Enthusiasm,"
from the Greek "entheos," meaning the God within. I did the
talk at the request of one of my newfound Charlotte friends,
Rick Matheney. Two years later when I was shopping for
groceries, someone who I didn't know stopped me in the
aisle and said, "You're the guy that gave that talk at the
Methodist Church on enthusiasm, aren't you?" "Yes I am,"
I said. He said, "I still think about that talk. It really impacted
me." I said, "Thank you very much."

As he walked away, my whole body became flush with
the thought of how much my words could impact and
encourage others. Interestingly, it came at the same time
I had begun to write a column for the *Charlotte Business
Journal*. It's amazing how acts of kindness can return to you
to be your own incentive, and your own encouragement,
to pursue your goals and dreams for success.

When you begin to give value
to the world, somehow the people
you affect will find a way to tell you.
Even if it takes a couple of years.

Your instincts will tell you what to do, but it's your personal
power that will actually create the deed. Start small. An
acorn, a tulip bulb, a mustard seed, or a kernel of corn.
Plant it, nurture it, and give it room to grow. If you just
water it regularly, in a year or two it will begin to blossom.

Master The Big 8.5 Elements of Positioning:
The art of becoming known as a valued authority

1. Getting in print. Use public relations to your maximum advantage. Get yourself mentioned, but not featured. If the story is about the customer or vendor then you become the hero to them.

2. Being published. My weekly article on sales, loyalty, and personal development has been published since 1992. It is the source of my notoriety, my books, my seminars, and my wealth.

3. Speaking in public. When you speak to a group, you're a presumed leader. You may not know the group, but when you're done, the whole group knows you.

4. Using the Internet to communicate value. My weekly e-zine, *Sales Caffeine*, reaches 130,000 people a week with a value message. Help others profit first, and your profit will last.

5. Taking an active role in your trade association. Get to know, and network with, others who count. Lead a group. Get involved. If you learn enough, eventually you can teach.

6. Being noticeably different. Look at the work shirt I present my seminars in. Risky outfit -- but it works. You don't have to be off the wall, but you must be slightly left or right of center or you'll blend in with the wallpaper.

7. Adding attraction to your outreach. Whenever you see an article of mine, you will also see an offer to go to my Web site to get more. (Like the free GitBit at the bottom of this page.) Whatever outreach you offer, give someone a reason to go to your Web site and get more.

8. Adding differentiation to your everyday business expressions. Your voice mail, your fax cover sheet, your proposal, and your business card all suck. What does that say about the greatness of you, your product, and your company? (Especially you.)

8.5 Letting others sell for you. The power of testimonials cannot be denied. Testimonials make your reputation. They make sales when you can't. And they give proof to the statements you make. Customers and prospects believe others like themselves more than they believe you.

Free Git✗Bit: **Want to check out my four page detailed description of power positioning to get known and how to be perceived as a person of value?** Go to www.gitomer.com, register if you are a first time user, and enter the word POSITION in the GitBit box.

What to do
with those you attract

WARNING: Once you begin to become attractive, not everyone who tries to make contact with you will be beneficial. My response to that is: Treat everyone who tries to make contact with you with respect and dignity. The same way that you would want someone to treat you if you were trying to connect with them. It's a universal law, probably better known as karma, or the world paying you back for what you do.

5

Here's what to do: CONTINUE TO GIVE THINGS AWAY.

In my lifetime, one of the most interesting and powerful elements of my own success has been giving things away to others -- without measuring. I have never given something to someone and told them, "You owe me one." I've always just given freely, without expectation. This way the world will pay me back or someone else in the world will pay me back tenfold. Sometimes the person will pay me back, but I consider it a surprise, or a gift, rather than a debt.

Getting in front of people who can say "Yes!" to you

If you're going to try to make a connection, doesn't it seem kind of logical that you would want to connect with those who could help you the most, right away?

Doesn't it also seem logical that you would want to be in front of as big of a prospect base as possible?

When I write my column, it appears in weekly business newspapers. A high percentage of the readers are salespeople, business executives, or entrepreneurs -- my exact target audience.

Here's the philosophy behind it:

I put myself in front of people who can say "Yes!" to me, and I deliver value first.

This has been my entire marketing strategy for the past fifteen years. People read my column, get to know my philosophy, read something that they like, perhaps pass it on to others, and then my phone rings.

Sometimes the phone rings with a request for more information. Sometimes the phone rings with a request for me to do a seminar.

But whatever it is, it's a lead; it's a connection, and a valuable one at that. I didn't connect with them. Hell, I didn't even know they existed. I just created a value message and they called.

Seems simple -- but it's not easy. Some people read for years before they call, so I need to have a different value message each week.

MAJOR AHA! Would those same people have called if I had simply placed an ad in the paper? An ad claiming "I'm the greatest sales trainer of all time." Doubtful. *Unless* the ad was an opportunity for them to come to one of my seminars *after* my column had appeared there, in the same position, for years.

Now you begin to understand the word VALUE, the law of attraction, and the power of consistency in front of your target audience -- the ones who can say "Yes!" to you.

I always find it amusing when someone tells me they have a list of people from their target audience, and their intention is to cold call them. That's somewhere between a poor joke and pathetic.

On a cold call you have to explain yourself, sell yourself, sell your company, sell your product, and face major rejection (major being defined as somewhere between 85 to 98 out of 100 -- that's pretty major).

If you would have taken the time to mail or e-mail those same one hundred people something of value (about them), some of them might have called you. And the ones that you decided to call would all take your call if you referenced the value piece you'd previously sent them.

> ### Identifying a target audience is easy. Knowing how to get in front of them is harder. But it makes selling yourself much easier than cold calling. It makes connecting so much easier when you have become somewhat known to your prospective connectee.

Go back to my weekly column for just one moment. It's in ninety-five business papers each week. Thousands of salespeople cut my column out and paste it on their office wall or keep it in a notebook. If I went around to any one of the cities where my column appears and began cold calling random businesses, odds are high that someone on the sales team reads my column, and saves it. They would be honored that I cold called them and would take me to their CEO in two seconds. I'm able to connect with them, or anyone in their company through them, because I delivered a consistent value message to them -- for years.

Think about the connections that you want to make. And instead of just figuring out a script and dialing a number, why don't you try to create a strategy and a game plan for getting in front of them with a value message instead of trying to get in front of them with a cold call.

What are the three secrets of getting known?
(HINT: writing, e-zine, speaking)

Throughout the course of this asset, I have drilled my "secrets of getting known" to make certain you know which three should have priority in your life, and which three will give you the highest probability of creating the law of attraction, building relationships, and creating a reputation -- to make it easy for you to connect.

I am going to repeat them here:

1. Writing. Writing does not just lead to connections. Writing does not just lead to the law of attraction. Writing does not just lead to clarifying your thoughts and philosophies. Writing does not just lead to articles and books. **Writing leads to wealth.**

SUCCESS ACTION: Set aside fifteen minutes a day when you first wake up and write. It's best if you have a laptop because you can correct as you go. Each morning pick a topic. It's easiest if you start out recounting a story. Something that happened with your pet, or maybe a travel experience. Maybe something that happened with your family. Each day you complete the file, store it in a writing folder and edit it again the following morning. You'll find all the flaws you couldn't find the morning you wrote it. Here's the editing secret: Don't just read it on the screen, read it out loud. Every flaw will appear as you speak it.

2. E-zine. I established *Sales Caffeine* in 2001. All I was trying to do was get a value message out to as many salespeople as I could to help them improve their sales. About six months later, I asked my subscribers to buy some of my books and products. They bought. Lots. I made a specific request in September of 2003. I asked them all to buy *The Sales Bible* in the new paperback edition. On September 3, 2003, *The Sales Bible* reached number one on www.amazon.com at two o'clock in the afternoon. At that time, I had approximately 50,000 subscribers. At this writing, I reach more than 130,000 subscribers each week. I wish I could tell you the true power of the e-mail magazine. I talk about it, actually I preach it, based on what it has brought me. It's not just my weekly sales message; it's how I stay in touch with more than 130,000 salespeople. And it's a technology that you can employ today.

> ### Over the next millennium, the single most valuable asset you and your company will possess is your e-mail mailing list. Build it, and guard it with your life.

5

SUCCESS ACTION: Create a list of twenty-six tips that your customers can use. You now have the basis for six months worth of weekly e-zines. Go to a college that has graphic design courses, and ask the instructor to create a class project to design your e-zine. You'll have over twenty-five incredible designs to pick from. Pay the winner $100, and give them a bottle of wine. Now gather all your e-mail names, put them in a file, edit your e-zine, paste it in an e-mail message – and hit the "send" button. Do that every week until you die.

3. Speaking. Just as writing leads to books, writing leads to speaking. The more you write, the more speech content you will amass. Then there's the matter of learning to speak in front of others, and gaining enough confidence to speak in front of others. Fortunately, they go hand in hand. The more speeches you give, the more confidence you build. The secret is being prepared. Contrary to popular belief and myth, people are not afraid to speak, they're just unprepared. Same with you. If your information is valuable, and you have one ounce of dynamic passion in your soul, your message will be well received and you will be perceived as a leader, as an expert, and eventually as an authority. **Continue to write and build your information base.**

SUCCESS ACTION: Call a Rotary Club or Kiwanis Club in your city. Find out the person's name in charge of booking speakers, and book a speech. That will force you to write the speech and practice the speech.

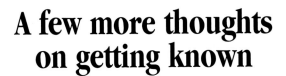

A few more thoughts on getting known

"Who knows you" can be measured. I have at least three people a day come up to me and want to talk sales, or tell me a story about a seminar of mine they went to, or get me to sign their book.

It's a nice feeling. It's also a report card.

It takes time. I started writing in March of 1992. My first book came out in November of 1994. Since 1992, I have delivered more than 1,800 speeches and seminars. And every one was a result of someone calling me: 1,800 booked engagements -- ZERO sales calls.

That's the power of writing.
That's the power of giving value first.
That's the result of getting in front of your audience with a value message.

MAJOR CLUE: It takes thought to create value. You have to decide to do it. *And* you have to dedicate the time to do it. I have seen this work first-hand. I did it. And so can you.

ASSET 6
THE SECRET POWER OF CONNECTIONS

1. The biggest connection mistake you can make!

2. In the Dallas airport

3. A group of connections. Harnessing the connection power of many

4. The power of friendliness

5. If you schmooze, you looze

6. WOW! them to WOO them (memorability *plus* value)

7. From MEOW to WOW! Lito gets a business card

8. Staying in touch. The E-ZINE

9. Rapport: Building it, and finding the link

10. The secret of turning contacts into relationships

11. The law and secrets of attraction

The biggest connection mistake you can make!

Anyone you meet is a connection. The challenge for you is to determine how each one fits into your asset base of human capital.

Casual connections, formal connections, business connections, referred connections, and networking alliances are all valuable.

MAJOR MISTAKE: The problem with people (not you of course) is that they tend to prejudge others. They spot the negative first -- what they don't like about them, not what they do like about them. This is a HUGE error in trying to connect.

Prejudging has played a major role in sales failure. Salespeople (not you of course) will often prejudge a person from the outside, continue the prejudgment through the presentation, and then look like a fool at the end when they have completely misread the other person.

The antidote to prejudgment is questioning. Asking the other person to reveal their intentions, their characteristics, and even their knowledge, will help anybody (you included) eliminate the fatal flaw of prejudging, so that you can build on one of the most powerful assets you possess: an open mind.

6

UNIVERSAL TRUTH
OF CONNECTING

Open Mind : Open Wallet
Closed Mind : Closed Wallet

-- Jeffrey Gitomer

6

In the Dallas airport

In 1982, after a big imprinted sportswear show, I was at the Dallas airport. I noticed a guy I had casually met from a T-shirt manufacturing company. He was swearing at the American Express money machine (pre ATM). It seems the machine ate his card. He looked desperate.

I walked over, reintroduced myself, found out the problem, and loaned him $100 so that he would have cash for the trip home. Two days later, he sent me a check for $100 and a thank you note.

Turns out he was the president of his company. Two months later, he called me and asked if I was interested in printing garments for the 1984 Olympics. He had the sublicense to manufacture from Levi's, and it just so happened we had a state-of-the-art printing facility. "Of course," I said. He gave me a contract to print every shirt -- 1,600,000 garments, $750,000 worth of business -- because I was paying attention at the airport. And because I was living my philosophy of "help other people."

NOTE WELL: I could have just as easily prejudged this guy as a fool banging a machine. All I did was take a closer look, and issue an ounce of trust. And all that happened is that I earned an opportunity and a ton of money.

6

A group of connections: Harnessing the connection power of many

I don't just join organizations -- I participate. And at some point, I lead. When I joined the Charlotte Chamber of Commerce, I was a member for two years, then I led a group of entrepreneurs called the "business growth network." I began to do new member orientations every month for the people who had just joined the chamber. I did that every month for four years and made more connections, and more friends, than I can count. I gave away things for free, but I also sold things, including my consulting services.

One day, a little Chinese lady came up to me and told me that she could get my new book, *The Sales Bible*, published in China. Less than two years later, the book was published and I had earned more than $100,000 in royalties -- as a result of giving a free speech at a chamber of commerce meeting.

In 1991, I joined MBC (Metrolina Business Council). About one hundred members, whose objective is to do business with one another. Within that group, I have made two dozen lifelong friends, and created dozens more solid business connections. The reason for my success is simple: I did my best to do business with (spend money with) as many members as I could. And I also did my best to get them business.

At each bi-monthly meeting of MBC, the opening twenty minutes is an opportunity for members to thank each other for business. My goal for each meeting is to thank five members, and *be thanked* by five members. For ten years, I have always achieved that goal.

Joining organizations is not an option, it's an imperative if you seek to make powerful connections.

The easiest way to measure your success is to measure your involvement. Once again, the rule of "the more, the more" comes into play. The more you get involved and the more you give to others, the more connections you will make, the more friendships you will garner, and ultimately, the more money you will earn.

IMPORTANT NOTE: If you go in doing it for the money, don't even bother to start. If you get involved looking to connect and help others, I promise you will win -- and your winnings will be far more than money.

6

The power of friendliness

Do you consider yourself a friendly person? Do you consider yourself a likeable person? Friendly and likeable go hand in hand. Look at the first page of this book: "All things being equal, people want to do business with their friends." Then look at the opposite page: "All things being not quite so equal, people STILL want to do business with their friends."

These two statements have a HUGE impact on making connections, getting referred connections, and maintaining connections. Friend is the root word of *friendly*. And friendly is a key to your success that cannot be measured.

Friendly is also an attitude. One that must be in constant "positive" so that all possible connections will be attracted to you. Maybe you can see it better through those at the opposite end of the spectrum. Think of people you know that are unfriendly, bitter, cynical, negative, and unkind. They are people you avoid like the plague.

CONNECTION EXERCISE: Make an effort today to be proactive-friendly. Compliment people at random. See if you can create ten smiles. It's easy to do. I do it all the time. It's like a friendly exercise. I flex my friendly muscle every day.

Free Git✗Bit: **Want to get things more friendly at work?** I have the formula AND the strategies for implementation. Go to www.gitomer.com, register if you are a first time user, and enter the word FRIENDLY into the GitBit box.

If you schmooze, you looze

There have been several books written on the art of schmoozing. To me, schmoozing is idle talk, gossip chatter, and other meaningless dialogue that will not get you what you want, and will often create an unfavorable impression of who you are and what your M.O. is.

Schmoozers tend to do anything but get to the point. Now don't get me wrong, football talk is great -- if both people are football fans. Business talk is great -- if both people are in business. But schmoozing tends to be one-sided, or wasted talk about the weather or the local news. People who "keep up with current affairs so they have something to talk about" have nothing of substance to talk about.

Maybe it would be better if I didn't condemn schmoozing altogether, but rather called it pointed schmoozing, focused schmoozing, engaging schmoozing, or meaningful schmoozing. Then you would understand it better, and the people who write books on schmoozing won't hate me forever.

If you're trying to make a genuine connection, then the key is to be perceived as a genuine person. This means having something of substance to say, saying it with confidence and authority, and doing it in a way that the other person is compelled to think and respond.

6

UNIVERSAL TRUTH
OF CONNECTING

**What you say to others
is a reflection of
who they think you are.**

**While you are speaking,
they are thinking and
deciding who you are,
whether they like you,
and whether they want to
take the next step with you.**

-- Jeffrey Gitomer

6

WOW! them to WOO them (memorability *plus* value)

When's the last time somebody said "WOW!" to you about something you did for them, or someone else?

Have you ever had "WOW!" done unto you? If you have, you'll never forget it.

I will never forget the day I checked into the Burbank Hilton Hotel and found that the staff, instead of giving the traditional fruit basket, had called my office, found out I collected sports memorabilia, and placed a baseball in my room -- autographed by thirty plus members of the hotel staff.

When will I throw that ball away? Answer: Never. Who will I show that ball to? Answer: Everybody. What did I say when I got that ball? I said, "WOW!" And I continue to say "WOW!" every time I retell the story.

WOO, WOO!

BEFORE YOU CAN WOO!, YOU GOTTA WOW!

JERK

ISN'T IT BOW-WOW?

6

Receiving a WOW! is often a combination, on the giver's part, of creativity, memorability, and personalization. Sometimes I do corporate events where they want me to wear the garment that they have chosen for the meeting. It's usually nice, but not something I'm going to wear more than once -- with the exception of three events over the past ten years:

1. The Florida Panthers gave me a hockey jersey with my name on the back and the number "1" on the jersey.

2. The Denver University hockey team gave me a personalized jersey. That jersey was autographed by the 2004 NCAA hockey champions. They gave me a jersey that had "GITOMER" on the back with the number "1."

3. I did a seminar for Rhino Courts. They make backyard basketball, tennis, and sport courts. They decided to have hockey jerseys made with their cool logo of a rhinoceros embroidered on the front, like a team logo. They asked me if I would wear the garment during my seminar. I said, "Sure." They gave me one that had "GITOMER" on the back of it and the number "1." During the break, they gave jerseys out to every attendee. And every jersey had the person's name on the back of it, along with the number "1." I have never heard so much **WOW!** in all my life. Remember the scene of the ping pong ball dropping on the mouse trap, and all the other mouse traps going pop, pop, pop, pop? That's what the Rhino Courts audience was like. Wows were popping up everywhere Wow! Wow! … Wow! Wow! Wow!

Every one of you has experienced a WOW! Very few of you have given one.

Almost no one makes a goal or a resolution at the beginning of the year that says: "I gotta WOW! more people." Bob Carr of TLC (sprinklers and outdoor lighting systems in Baltimore, Maryland) is the only person I know with a "WOW! budget." He spends a hundred dollars a week wowing one customer at random. He'll install an outdoor light that turns on when you drive up your driveway, or a timing device on a sprinkler. It's a $5,200 budget that will earn him hundreds of thousands of dollars in business and fifty-two lifetime fans a year. In ten short years, Bob will have 520 loyal fans -- otherwise known as loyal salespeople -- on his team. (Unless of course he doubles his budget.)

Do you have a $5,200 "WOW! budget?" It's a hell of a lot less than your beer budget.

The power of WOW! cannot be understated. WOW! leads to loyalty, referred business, and word of mouth advertising. WOW! creates reputation in the most positive of ways, and gives prospective customers anticipation that a WOW! may be bestowed upon them if they do business with you.

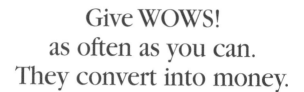

Give WOWS!
as often as you can.
They convert into money.

My business card is a coin. I give away about 20,000 of them a year. Everyone who ever gets one says some form of "WOW!" Something like, "WOW, this is the coolest card I have ever seen!" or "Hey, Bill, come here! You gotta see this card!" There is no "WOW!" in that sentence, but it certainly is implied.

When I give my coin away, there are two guarantees. **GUARANTEE NUMBER ONE:** No one will ever throw it away, and **GUARANTEE NUMBER TWO:** Everyone I give it to will show it to someone else. We get hundreds of requests a year by mail or e-mail from those wanting one of my business cards. My coin card has created instant memory, instant favorable impression, and instant "WOW!" to everyone who receives it.

How many people are calling and asking for one of your cards?

Some of you are whining as you read this because you either don't have, or can't afford, a coin card. Even more of you are whining about the fact that your company won't let you alter your boring card. Answer: Create your own card.

From MEOW to WOW!
Lito gets a business card

On page 120, I told you that when I first moved to Charlotte in 1988, I was low on funds. Okay, I was broke. I had someone design up a sheet of business cards in PageMaker on my computer. I could print them out at Kinko's on good cardstock and cut them up -- at very low cost. I didn't have very many employees. Okay, I had two employees. But they had cards in under an hour.

One day, I decided to give my pet cat, Lito, a business card. I gave her the title, "Corporate Mascot." She played a vital role in my office productivity. Whenever I needed an important paper, Lito was lying on it.

The minute I started to give Lito's card out, word in the Charlotte business community spread like wildfire. "Gitomer's cat has a business card!" Everywhere I went, people would ask if I had one of my cat's business cards with me. I always did. I wrote an article about it. Hundreds of requests came in for one of Lito's cards. Everyone who got her card kept it, showed it to someone else, talked about it, and talked about me.

I was at a networking event in Charlotte when a Fast 50 corporate president ran over to me saying, "Hey, Gitomer, show this guy your cat's card." "Have one," I said, "and have one of mine in case the cat isn't in. I usually handle her calls."

That was fourteen years ago. Even though Lito passed away in 2002, and I haven't given out her card in years, I still get an occasional request for one.

MAJOR CLUE: My point here is not that my cat had a card. My point is that I used a little creativity, and spent under $20 to create WOW!, and so can you.

Anything memorable will help you connect.

YOUR CAT HAS A BUSINESS CARD?! WHAT ABOUT MY NEEDS?

Staying in touch.
The E-ZINE

The value of an e-zine (also known as an e-mail magazine) cannot be denied or overlooked as a critical way to stay in touch, and provide value to every connection, every week.

PLEASE NOTE: I am not an expert at e-zines, but I'm getting there. And, I am making money with my e-zine -- but that's NOT why I send it out every week.

I send it out because it's my weekly value message to more than 130,000 people. Do you get it? Go to www.gitomer.com and look for the icon that asks you to subscribe. Do it now! You'll get this week's copy right away, and you can refer to it as you read this chapter.

HISTORY: In the year 2000 (before 9/11), the economy was starting to tank. I wanted to stay in front of my customers with a value message. I decided to try e-mail. Easy, fast, cheap, and readily available.

I believed both the construction and design would be critical to its success. I used graphics created by my designers, coded it in HTML, found a list host, put the great Traci Capraro in charge of it, loaded it up with value-information, and hit the "send" button.

6

I used my in-house customer list as a starting point: 21,000 people received the first edition of *Sales Caffeine* on November 13, 2001.

The goal was to help my customers get better at sales during an economic slump. We polled 1,000 of our customers and found out where they needed help. For almost six years, I've answered my customers' needs and concerns by responding to questions, providing answers, and talking about and providing sales ideas. Ideas from me, from other experts, and from readers.

Sales Caffeine not only offers timely and real-world advice, it also broadcasts sales success stories and boosts confidence in beginning, intermediate, and the advanced "I-know-it-all-already" salespeople.

With my faithful column followers and growing customer database, the circulation list and content provided within each e-zine grew and expanded to its current state.

In 250 issues the list of subscribers has grown to 130,000. There has been a major design change to the e-zine year after year. My team and I are now working on a Web site dedicated to *Sales Caffeine* and its archives.

DID I ENCOUNTER ANY PROBLEMS? Well, unless you consider server crashes, list blockage, wrong list service provider, technical glitches, and an assortment of other "people's inadequacies" a problem – then no – we have had no problems – only opportunities to build *Sales Caffeine* to one of the most subscribed to and respected information instruments in the world of sales. And I'm shooting for one million subscribers in the next three years.

THE QUESTION IS: How can you prepare your own professional e-zine? One that helps you preserve the loyalty of your present customers, provides a path to new customers, and generates new revenue?

Here are a few examples of what your message of help and support needs to be:

IF YOU SUPPLY A PRODUCT LIKE A COPIER OR A COMPUTER:
You want to stress productivity, profitability, image, and morale – the things that the use of your machine creates. You may also want to give tips related to sales and service.

IF YOU ARE A SERVICE LIKE ACCOUNTING:
You want to talk money, tax advantages, sales, and service.

IF YOU ARE AN ADD-ON LIKE HEALTH INSURANCE:
It's all about health, prevention, diet, food, wellness, and the things that breed life.

THE KEY IS TO PROVIDE:

- **Information that others perceive as valuable.**

- **Information that's helpful to them.**

- **Information that helps them build their business.**

- **Information that helps them make a profit or increase productivity.**

ASK YOURSELF THESE 5.5 QUESTIONS:

1. How much are my present customers worth, and what am I willing to invest to keep them, and keep my competition from stealing them?

2. How much is a new customer worth, and how am I staying in front of them after my presentation?

3. How am I differentiating myself from my competition? Would an e-zine help me? (There's an easy answer to this one: Suppose your competition started a real slick e-zine tomorrow. How would you feel?)

4. How am I staying in front of my customers -- the lifeblood of my business -- with a value message? A message that makes me different from, and better than, my competition?

5. How professional do I want my e-zine to look?

5.5 How important is it for me to be in front of my customers, and how am I doing that now?

Free Git✗Bit: **Want more information on building your own e-zine?** Go to www.gitomer.com, register if you are first time user, and enter the word E-ZINE in the GitBit box.

UNIVERSAL TRUTH
OF CONNECTING

Communicate VALUE
to EVERY connection,
EVERY week.

-- *Jeffrey Gitomer*

6

Rapport: Building it, and finding the link

Rapport is defined with several words: relation, connection, accord, harmony, and agreement. Rapport is a subtle yet significant aspect of the connection process.

If you find common interests with a prospective connection, you can establish a business friendship. People are more likely to buy from a friend than a salesman.

What do you do to establish rapport? Are you sharp enough to find something in common besides business after you open the conversation?

CONCEPT 1: Establish rapport when working a room.

Establishing rapport with a prospect at a networking event enhances your ability to connect. Just follow these guidelines to maximize your productivity at (and after) a networking event:

IF YOU ALREADY KNOW THE PERSON ... And you have a business agenda, discuss it within two minutes. If they're talking to someone you don't know, get introduced and see if there is a fit for you. If the known person is your customer, spend a couple of minutes building the personal relationship by trying to establish mutual interests. If you make a promise or commitment, get another card from the person and IMMEDIATELY write it down on the back. No matter what, after five minutes...MOVE ON.

IF YOU DON'T KNOW THE PERSON … Give your 30-second personal commercial and then ask what he or she does. Don't elaborate or try to sell until the other person has talked about themselves, *and* you have tried to establish mutual interest. Ask an open-ended question about how they now use your type of product or service, such as where are you presently getting…how are you using…who are you buying from…what's been your experience…

Questions that will engage the prospect, create dialogue, make them talk about themselves, and make them begin to open up and reveal themselves, are the types you need to ask. As soon as they broach a personal issue, grab it and expand on it.

When you engage a prospect, try to find out their personal interests. After the traditional exchange of business information, try to find out what the prospect does after work, or what they're doing next weekend. You might even try out a couple of interest items if an event is near or just passed, like a ball game, car race, concert, play, or business function.

After you have gotten to know a little about this person, you can now begin the "let's get together later to finish this discussion" part that will solidify the all-important appointment.

Be careful not to spend too much time on subjects of mutual interest. It's tempting to spend thirty minutes talking about things you like. Don't. Your opportunity to meet others awaits you. You can expand the conversation at a lunch next week. Move on to other prospects.

6

NOTE: Write furiously on the back of their business card. Be sure to include anything personal you spoke about, so you can begin the appointment where you left off at the networking event.

If you are able to establish rapport when networking, you will have a perfect conversation item when you follow up to make an appointment.

CONCEPT 2: Establish rapport on the phone.

*Now let's look at rapport on the phone…*It's likely that you're calling to make an appointment or some kind of follow-up, so focus on three things:

1. Get to the point in 15-seconds. If it's a cold call, begin to establish rapport by getting to the point! State the purpose of your call immediately. It's not necessary (and often a put-off) to ask the insincere, "How are you today?" Just state your name, your company name, and how you can help the prospect. Once you've done that, there is a sense of relief from both sides. The prospect is relieved because he now knows why you've called. And you're relieved because the prospect hasn't hung up on you. Now you can go about the task of establishing some rapport, and setting the appointment.

2. Be happy and humorous. Is the prospect formal or friendly? Try to use humor at least twice during the conversation (but don't force it). People love to laugh. A quick, clean, one-minute story or original joke can do more for buyer rapport than ten minutes worth of sales talk.

3. Get to know something personal about the prospect. You can also gain insight by questioning, then listening. Prospect mood, hometown, and personality will all be revealed in just a few minutes on the phone. Listen for, and be sensitive to, the mood of the prospect. If he or she is short or gruff, just say, "I can tell you're busy (or not having the best of days). Why don't we pick a time more convenient for me to call."

I also listen closely for speech accent. It gives you a clue where the prospect is from, and it's a great subject if you're well traveled or from the same place.

Sell the appointment with a personal touch. For example, if you're talking to a basketball fan you might say: "I know I can help you reach your computer training needs. With a ten minute appointment, I can show you how we can help you in the first five minutes and have the other five to discuss who the Pistons should draft."

CONCEPT 3: Establish rapport when meeting someone face-to-face, one-on-one.

The rapport opportunity on an appointment in the prospect's office is the easiest place to establish rapport.

LOOK FOR CLUES AS SOON AS YOU WALK INTO THE PROSPECT'S PLACE OF BUSINESS. Pictures, plaques or awards on the wall, magazines subscribed to that don't match the business. When you get in the prospect's office, look for pictures of children or events, bookcase items, books, diplomas, awards, desk items, or anything that reveals personal likes or after-business pursuits. Ask about an award or trophy. Ask, "How did you win that?" and the floodgates of personal

information will open up. Ask about a diploma or picture. Your prospect will be glad to talk about what he or she just did or likes to do.

FIND SOMETHING IN COMMON AS THEY TALK. Try to engage him or her in intelligent conversation with open-ended questions about the interests you have in common. It's better if you're well-versed in the subject, but the object is to get the prospect to talk about what makes them happy. If you can get the prospect to laugh, it will set the stage for a positive connection.

BEWARE OF THE FAILURE TO EMPHASIZE RAPPORT WHEN THE PROSPECT COMES TO YOUR PLACE OF BUSINESS. It is more difficult to establish common ground because you don't have the advantage of the telling items that would be present in their surroundings. So...be observant. Look at clothing, car, rings, imprinted items, their business card, or anything that gives you a clue as to the type of person they are.

BE FRIENDLY. Ask open-ended questions just below the surface. Surface questions or talk, such as the weather or "Did you find the place OK?" should be avoided at all costs. Try to find out what they did last weekend, or what they're doing this weekend. Ask about a movie or a book. Avoid politics, their personal problems, and for goodness sakes, don't lament your personal problems.

PEOPLE LOVE TO TALK ABOUT THEMSELVES. Ask the right question and it's tough to shut them up. The object is not to get them to talk, the object is to get them to reveal. The object is for you to find a subject, idea, or situation that you BOTH know about, or are interested in.

ONE LAST WORD OF CAUTION: Budget your time establishing rapport. You're on a mission: Make a value connection. But I can assure you the mission is most likely to be accomplished if you have made a friend before you make the presentation.

If you establish common ground
with the other person,
they will like you, believe you,
begin to trust you,
and connect with you
on a deeper level.
A "things-in-common" level.

The best way to win
the connection is to
first win the person.

This information about establishing rapport can also be found in question 77 of The Little Red Book of Sales Answers, *and will appear in several other books until you finally understand the importance and the power of rapport.*

6

The secret of turning contacts into relationships

Here are the fundamentals of doing all you can to ensure that a contact blossoms into a relationship.

- **Figure out who they are, and what they want.**

- **Determine your compatibility with them.**

- **Find out how you can help them get what they want.**

- **Begin dialogue on a regular basis that has information they can use.**

- **Try to learn more about them as time progresses.**

- **Realize and be aware that people reveal their true selves over time.**

- **Pay close attention to signs, and follow your instincts.**

- **Do what you say you'll do.**

- **Make sure they know your needs and desires.**

HERE IS THE SECRET: The more they like you, and feel they receive value from you, the more likely it is that the relationship will grow and prosper. Before you can take, you gotta give.

UNIVERSAL TRUTH
OF CONNECTING

The real rule of "give and take" is: Before you can take, you gotta give.

-- Jeffrey Gitomer

6

The law and secrets of attraction

The title looks alluring, but what I'm about to reveal is not a secret. It's a process. The secret is: Very few people are willing to do it. That's GREAT news for you, IF you're willing to work hard, and keep at it for years. Another secret is that results are slow, and many get discouraged. So discouraged that they quit. Yep, they quit just before they get to the gold. Start, stick at it, and never quit.

THE LAW OF ATTRACTION IS:

Put yourself in front of people who can say "Yes!" to you, and deliver value first.

HERE'S THE "LAW OF ATTRACTION" FORMULA:

- **Gather your value and valuable information, and commit to it in writing.**

- **List places where you could appear in person, and in print, that would impact existing customers and prospects.**

- **Expose yourself on all fronts.**

- **Once you have appeared in print and in person, and have been able to expose your ideas one-on-one, it's time to say them to a group.**

- **Once your exposure begins, your attraction seeds are planted. Your response is based on how well you water and maintain your garden.**

Save and savor your connections.

At the end of my weekly column is a feature called the GitBit. It's a major part of my attraction. People read my column (my value message) down to the last sentence, and then they go to my Web site to get the free GitBit. They are fans, or avid salespeople, or both. By offering more value to the column, I am able to attract *and* identify who my readers are.

If you're trying to attract your market through writing, make certain that you give them a valuable reason to take additional action. I offer more value on the subject that my readers have just read about. So should you.

ASSET 6.5

THE VALUE OF CONNECTIONS

1. The myth of
"Six Degrees of Separation"

2. Your new blood type:
N+ (Networking Positive)

3. Finding the LINK and
deepening the connection

4. The secret of NetWeaving™

5. Developing strategic
alliance referrals: Hard,
but WOW!

6. Building your circle of
influence and multiplying
your connection power

The myth of "Six Degrees of Separation"

The theory was first proposed in 1929 by the Hungarian writer, Frigyes Karinthy, in a short story called *Chains*. The theory said that you can reach anyone by going through six people. Someone who knows someone else, who knows someone else, who knows someone else, who knows someone else, who knows the president of the United States -- or someone even more powerful -- Howard Stern.

If you have to go through six degrees of who, who, who, who, who, who -- the likelihood of getting to that final person is zero.

If you're trying to make
a big connection,
or any connection for that matter,
there has to be a valuable
or engaging reason for them
to want to connect with you.
That can eliminate all degrees.

I believe that you have one or two chances to do this -- not three, and certainly not six.

6.5

If you're looking to make that one connection, the first and best thing to do is look to your inner circle. Look at the most powerful people you know personally, or the most connected people you know personally, and see if you can limit the degrees of connection down to one degree. By doing this, you are more likely to connect, especially if your one-degree person is a friend of his or hers, and can personally recommend you.

HERE'S THE FORMULA:

The fewer degrees of separation there are, the more likely you can connect.

CONNECTION EXERCISE: Make a list of five people you would like to connect with. Next to each name, put the ONE PERSON you're certain can help you make the connection. To complete this exercise, you have to do two things: create the engaging reason or value proposition for each person that you want to meet with, and then make five phone calls.

Your new blood type: N+ (Networking Positive)

The lifeblood of connecting, and the nurturing of relationships, stems from networking. It is the pure spring water from which an endless flow of people bubble up.

Networking is your life skills and social skills combined with your business skills.

It's *business leisure* conducted before and after work -- as opposed to business frantic, which is conducted from nine to five (the exception being lunch).

To maximize your networking effectiveness, you must follow one simple rule. RULE A1A:

To be successful at networking, go where your customers and prospects go, or are likely to be.

6.5

Networking is a mandatory function of business for salespeople, entrepreneurs, and everyone in every segment of commerce and career networks. Scientists, electrical engineers, and surgeons all have their annual meeting of some kind, where they get together and "talk shop." Giant trade shows attract buyers and sellers from all over the world.

People who attend important business events have unlimited networking opportunities. They socialize, they fraternize, they attend the mandatory events, but they don't know how to take advantage of the relationship-building opportunities and the business-building opportunities laid there right in front of them. A large percentage of the people attending look at it as a three-day party.

The object of any networking event is to make a lasting connection, not create a lasting bad impression.

Free Git✗Bit: **Want a list of the 21.5 best places to network?** It appears in my book, *The Little Red Book of Selling*, but you can also get it on my Web site. Go to www.gitomer.com, register if you are a first time user, and enter the word PLACES in the GitBit box.

IF NETWORKING AND CONNECTING ARE REALLY IN YOUR BLOOD, THEN ALCOHOL SHOULD NOT BE.

DOES BUDWEISER HAVE ANY ALCOHOL IN IT?

Finding the LINK and deepening the connection

Think about what you love to do, think about where you grew up, and think about where you have traveled. Now think about where you went to school, what your favorite sports teams are, and what sports you like to play. These are personal things to you. Passions.

When you are connecting with others, keep in mind that they have passions too.

If you have matching passions, or can in other ways make a link with the other person, the connection goes from casual to personal.

I get booked for about 120 seminars a year. I schedule a one-hour pre-seminar conference call with every customer, so that I can personalize my talk for their business. When I saw Shea Commerical on my schedule for a pre-seminar conference call, I never gave it a second thought.

6.5

I began in my normal manner, trying to ascertain information as to who would be at the conference, and what the theme of the meeting was. Jim Riggs, founder and CEO of the company, is a successful office condominium developer in Phoenix, Arizona. As we were talking, I detected a regional accent in his speech that told me he was from Philly. "Where'd you grow up?" I asked. "Just outside of Philadelphia," he said. "Really?" I said, "So did I. What city did you grow up in?" "Haddonfield," he said. "Really?" I said, "So did I. What street did you live on?" "Kings Highway," he said. "Really?" I said, "So did I. What number on Kings Highway?" "143 West," he said. "Really?" I said, "I grew up at 148 Kings Highway."

Turns out he grew up across the street from me. (About fifteen years after I lived there.) But his father was an OB-GYN who had delivered almost every baby in town, including a bunch of my friends. "My father will be at the seminar. He's one of my investors," he told me.

From the moment he said Haddonfield, even though I had never met or seen Jim Riggs personally, we were best of friends. We spent the next twenty minutes talking about Haddonfield High School, the wrestling team, the lousy football team, naming all the businesses and luncheonettes where we had eaten or been, and basically building a bond through our common link: Haddonfield, New Jersey.

When I finally met him, it was no different. Friends at first sight. And his dad was just as cool.

UNIVERSAL TRUTH
OF CONNECTING

**The worst way to get a referral
is to ask for one
right after you make a sale,
but before you have performed.**

**A good way to get a referral is
to ask for one after you have
delivered value to a customer.**

**A better way to get a referral
is to earn one.**

**The BEST way to get a referral
is to GIVE one.**

-- Jeffrey Gitomer

.5

The secret of NetWeaving™

As an impressionable youth, I watched my dad bring people together that he thought could "do business."

"What do you get from it, Pop?" I asked. "Nothing and everything, son. They don't pay me, but I am often rewarded by them or others in many ways," he said. "But I don't get it, Pop." "If you give to others without measuring, you get repaid without ever asking for it," he stated as though it were a law of the universe. "Oh," I said, without really understanding. "You'll get it later, son," he promised.

My dad repeated his philosophy for years, helping others at every turn and bringing people together. And he was often rewarded.

By osmosis, I have done the same thing. Never really thought about the right or wrong of it. Never even questioned the validity of it. Just did it. And I, too, have often been rewarded. Very often.

I later came to find that someone had named the philosophy NetWeaving™. Bob Littell, from Atlanta, has even written a book about it (www.netweaving.com). Cool.

Bob invited me to be the guest of honor at two NetWeaving™ events. One public event, held after one of my seminars. The other, a more private, small event held the next evening at an upscale location.

There were about 150 people putting a spin on the traditional networking process at the first event. "What can I do for you?" rather than, "What can you do for me?" Great concept. And it worked. After a brief lesson and introduction to the concept of NetWeaving™, people were engrossed so deeply that no one wanted to leave.

The second, smaller event was held at the fabulous SPA Sydell. An incredible day spa in midtown Atlanta that puts a new meaning to the word pamper. It's scientific skin care combined with spa services of every description.

About fifty people of influence and character (I guess that includes me) came together to see what they could do for one another. The results were fantastic. People spent hours trying to involve themselves in other's needs. To give of themselves first.

Wanna NetWeave? Start with your BEST. Your best friends, your best contacts, your best influencers, and even your best prospects. Throw a party. Doesn't have to be big. More like a gathering with a message and a mission: **Help others first.**

The good news is that people who think it's a crazy idea won't show. The better news is that everyone who does show for the event will be eager to participate. The best news is that you will have business opportunities being thrown at you left and right.

Think about the power of it. In traditional networking, you show up to "work the room" and try to make a few contacts. At a NetWeaving™ event, all the people in the room are trying to make connections for you. Wow!

In a nutshell, NetWeaving™ is connecting people, and positioning yourself as a resource to others -- often on a totally gratuitous basis -- with the *belief* that "what goes around, comes around."

The interesting part is that when you become involved in NetWeaving™, you get into a new business frame of mind. It makes you aware of the needs of others and at the same time challenges you to draw on your full range of contacts. The challenge is as great as the reward.

Like anything else, you have to practice the process outside the event in order to master it. Bob Littell is the current master. He's an insurance guy who doesn't sell insurance. He creates opportunities for other people to succeed, and then people buy from him.

Proof? I've seen it personally. And in two NetWeaving™ events, I saw more power than I've ever seen in a room. Not necessarily powerful people, rather people with the power to help others. It's a business sight to see. And when someone offers their help, you can't help but want to help others.

My philosophy of business has always been **GIVE VALUE FIRST**. People read my column and want more. Been doing that for eleven extremely successful years. Plan to continue that process for the next twenty-five years or so, and then I'll quit. The net result of my column is that I make hundreds of friends by helping them. Friends that one day may turn into business. That's NetWeaving™.

Developing strategic alliance referrals: Hard, but WOW!

"Jeffrey, what's the secret to getting more referrals?"
"Easy, *give* more referrals!"

SECRET TO REFERRALS: Give first, get second.

TWO BIG QUESTIONS:
1. Are you willing to refer your clients or customers to someone else?
2. Is someone else willing to refer their clients or customers to you?

ONE BIG ANSWER: Yes, if there is mutual trust. If no, stop reading this right now -- keep cold calling.

The big picture philosophy for "easy" referral success in your business is "strategic alliance referrals." Here are the prerequisites:

- **Your philosophy of sales is "build relationships."**
- **You consider yourself one of the best at what you do.**
- **You do a great (memorable) job in making the sale.**
- **You do a perfect job of delivering what you promised.**

.5

- You provide impeccable service after the sale.

- You are willing to do things with your customers to help them build THEIR business.

- You are well liked and respected.

- You are willing to get involved in the community.

This process came about by accident. I was doing a lot of business with a trademark attorney, registering various words and slogans. As our relationship matured and we became better friends, I began to refer clients from my consulting practice to him for patents and trademarks -- and he began referring his clients who wanted patents, but were without marketing and selling skills, to me. The perfect alliance was born. From there, I expanded it to include other businesses and civic activities, and my referrals shot through the roof.

Strategic alliance referrals doesn't just mean asking for referrals -- it's also earning referrals by working with your customers, other businesses, and community-based civic organizations, to help everyone benefit.

It's a game plan
to involve others,
so that everyone benefits.
Especially you.

What are some benefits of this concept? How are alliances used?

1. For credibility. To give your company more credibility, align yourself with the chamber of commerce, partner or joint venture with a big firm, or donate part of your proceeds to a charitable organization in exchange for using their name with your promotion.

2. To boost sales, make an impression, or get an audience. Align with a business that will deliver a gift of what they do at a reduced cost in exchange for the opportunity to make a sales call on your prospect or customer. It looks like you're the hero, and your ally gets a valuable lead. Look for companies who sell office plants, flowers, ad specialties, tickets, or gift baskets.

3. To get to the decision makers. Look to align yourself with someone already doing business with your targets. These are your best prospects for an alliance.

4. To get leads faster. Look at what steps it takes to get to your sale. Talk to people who sell your prospect before your sale is possible. Excellent candidates are contractors, equipment sellers, movers, or supply companies. Select vendors who are needed by the prospect before your product or services are needed.

5. To generate new prospects. Build your business network by joining leads clubs, business clubs, and professional associations.

6. To build business with existing customers and expand within that industry. Join their trade association or the chamber of commerce.

Finding, establishing, and developing strategic alliances and referral partners will get you more business than you can handle. But it doesn't just happen:

- **You must make and implement a strategic plan.**

- **You must establish (earn) mutual trust with everyone.**

- **You must be proactive in contacting and forming your alliances.**

- **You must be willing to give first -- and give without measuring or keeping score.**

- **You must allow time for these alliances to mature.**

- **You must be creative at what you do and how you do it.**

When you get a referral, someone is putting their own reputation on the line. They're saying, "I trust you enough to let you get involved with people who affect my career, my reputation, and my livelihood." It's a big responsibility. Giving and getting a referral means someone is willing to take a risk. Are you worth it?

Free Git✗Bit: **Want the blueprint for building referral alliances?** Go to www.gitomer.com, register if you are a first time user, and enter the word REFERRAL in the GitBit box.

Building your circle of influence and multiplying your connection power

Everybody has a circle of friends. People who you spend time with. People who come over to your house. People who you pray with. People who you play sports with. People who you socialize with. People who you do business with. There may be different people in each of those groups. In fact, it's most likely that none of the same people are in all of your groups.

CONNECTION EXERCISE: Take a moment and make a list of the twenty-five people that you call on, or that call on you, in times of need. Most of the time it's one-on-one connection. But how powerful would it be if you could interconnect them all? WOW!

Here's how: send an e-mail to everyone on your list. Introduce yourself -- and them to each other. Tell them that, from time to time, you'll be e-mailing all of them for ideas, with ideas, for connections that you need to make, and with connections that you have just made. Tell them that you will be asking for their help, and proactively offering help, in order to help build this alliance. Encourage others to respond in kind to you when needed. Also encourage others to add their twenty-five people to the list. If everyone does it, you'll have a closed network of 625 powerful people, 600 of whom you don't know, but any one of whom might provide you with the one thing you need, at the exact moment you need it. Is that powerful, or what?

6.5

UNIVERSAL TRUTH
OF CONNECTING

Most people have powerful connections.

Very few people have harnessed the power of their connections.

-- Jeffrey Gitomer

.5

EPILOGUE
CONNECTION MASTERY

1. Building the brand of YOU: Creating an image and a reputation

2. How to make the most important connections

3. Keeping a connection for the long term

4. Indirect connection: Connecting with clothing

5. The first class factor

6. The secret and power of "give value first"

7. The lifelong connection process

STOP!

Don't even think about doing anything in this section until you have high competency in the previous 6.5 assets of connecting.

YOU CAN READ IT...BUT DON'T TRY TO DO CALCULUS BEFORE YOU CAN ADD AND SUBTRACT.

The reason I'm telling you not to try this before you master the other elements is the same reason math teachers don't teach calculus before they teach addition and subtraction. One is a derivative of the other. Connecting is a progressive science that you learn over time.

You can't connect with Bill Gates until you've learned how to connect and build solid relationships with members of your local business community. If, and when, you ever get to Bill Gates's office, then you won't act like a fool and blow what could potentially be the biggest opportunity of your life.

My personal belief has always been that getting in the door is easy. The hard part is leaving with what you want.

Too often people make a goal of meeting someone, rather than meeting someone and having an objective or an agenda when they enter.

Building the brand of YOU: Creating your image and your reputation

Personal branding is not complicated, unless you take a course in it. Then it's scary as hell. Entrepreneurial personal branding and marketing is much easier.

I have a brand. Or should I say: *I AM the brand*. I have taken my name (Gitomer and Jeffrey Gitomer), and turned it into my brand. My column has been in the *Charlotte Business Journal* every week for eleven years. It's now in 95 markets, and growing. My Web site is my name: www.gitomer.com. My company is my name: Buy Gitomer. And everything I do has my name on it. (I even registered the URLs for the misspellings of my name.)

What's your brand? Not just your company brand -- I'm talking about your *personal* brand. In sales, prospects buy the salesperson FIRST. If they buy brand you, then they may buy what you're selling.

How do you get a brand? How do you create a brand?

First, if you're a small business person, don't read a book on it. I have yet to find one that is pragmatic enough to work. Second, think "me" and "give-to-get." Third, think "promotion combined with advertising." And the kicker -- it's **how hard you work, how smart you work,** and **how dedicated you are, combined with your self-belief, that will help your brand proliferate more that anything**.

Personal branding is...

• Creating demand for your product or service indirectly. (Through means other than direct advertising.)

• Getting the business community to have confidence in you -- as a respected, high-caliber individual.

• Getting the business community to have confidence in your business -- and earning a reputation for quality performance so good, that it's talked about.

• Establishing yourself as an expert. Why just be *in* the field, when you can be perceived *on top* of it?

• Being seen, and being known, as a leader. Standing in front of the group, and telling them. Or getting involved in a group and leading them. Showing up where everyone is, all the time.

• Being known as an innovator. Being known as a person or business of value. Being known as a resource.

• Separating yourself from your competition. Getting in front of the pack and setting a standard.

• Gaining professional stature. Your image is determined by others. Your outreach determines your image.

• Building your personal image, and the image of your business by being a consistent and positive performer, by associating with quality things and people, and by delivering what you promise. Getting talked about in a positive way.

• Making your phone ring with qualified prospects as a result of your total branding and marketing outreach, and converting those calls into sales.

HERE'S THE SECRET: *Become known as a person of action.*

The result of these actions will be a person who is known for getting things done -- a leader. It's not just a reflection on you, it's a reflection on your company, the products and services you offer, and your personal brand. It's something you can't place a value on, or buy, but it's the difference between sale and no sale. And the difference between having to sell, and people wanting to buy.

The result of these actions will be a brand new you.

Free Git✗Bit: **Want to know my personal formula for developing a personal brand?** Go to www.gitomer.com, register if you're a first time user, and enter the words PERSONAL BRAND in the GitBit box.

How to make the most important connections

The least understood element of connecting is that it's a two way street. You always want to connect with someone else.

But a bigger question is, do they want to connect with you?

If you are unable to connect, don't blame the other person for your inability to make it happen. There's always a way to connect. You just haven't found it yet. You just haven't earned it yet.

So ask yourself:

1. Why am I making this connection?

2. How am I going to make this connection?

3. Why would this person want to connect with me?

3.5 How am I going to keep this connection once I've made it?

Once you make the connection, and both parties are interested, you must keep the connection. That's the valuable part.

THE TWO KEYS: There are two key elements in connecting. Number one is: your preparation. Knowing who you're calling, knowing a little bit about their business, knowing what you want to accomplish on the first connection, and how you're going to make it happen.

Are you trying to set an appointment -- or make a sale? If you're trying to make an appointment, then don't try to make a sale. Make some notes about what you want to say in order to make the connection happen.

Number two is: have an objective to connect, and a reason that the other person might be interested. And make sure that they make sense. You may want to connect with me, but why would I want to connect with you?

Free Git✗Bit: Wondering whether it's better to send a letter or make a phone call for the initial connection? Go to www.gitomer.com, register if you're a first time user, and enter the words INITIAL CONNECTION in the GitBit box.

Keeping a connection for the long term

There are several elements that must be fully utilized in order to maintain meaningful long-term connections.

FIRST, there must be some intellectual or emotional attraction.

SECOND, there needs to be some common ground established that is of mutual interest to pursue.

THIRD, there must be some commitment to regular communication that has a "give" to it, rather than an "ask." (In other words, don't be calling your connection to consistently ask for favors. It gets old. And one day, your calls will go unreturned.)

And **FOURTH**, there must be occasional face-to-face meetings.

I belong to the National Speakers Association. I have many friends there, some of whom I only see once or twice a year. Most of them subscribe to my weekly e-mail magazine, or read my column in one of their local business papers. Occasionally I will get an e-mail or a phone call from one of them. All of them are my friends, and spending three or four days at the national convention or the winter workshop is enough to keep the friendship intact. We all have the speaking business in common. And everyone (me included) is looking to build that business. Most of the discussions focus on those issues. And of course there are those anecdotes of what went right and what went wrong that we each share an understanding of.

Each year, I try to deepen my relationship with existing friends and make three new friends in the association. I have been doing this for eleven years.

The number of significant long-term connections you keep can usually be counted on one or two hands.

Interestingly, I have probably just made you think of several people that you need to reconnect with. Someone you lost touch with, or should be keeping in touch with, but don't. I just thought of a few myself.

Long-term connections require a discipline, a self-discipline, as well as the preexisting friendship and the link.

NOTE WELL: It's not up to the other person to keep up the communication. It's up to you.

Indirect connection: Connecting with clothing

By connecting with hundreds of people, you'll learn by experience what works for you, and what doesn't work for you. You'll build your personality and your system of engagement. You'll come to understand methods that work, and methods that don't work. You'll also develop a style. A manner. How you carry yourself in public. Your image. But you may not understand how you're perceived by others.

When I first moved to Charlotte, my image was dungarees, a Ralph Lauren shirt, and a tie. After about a year, a businessman came over to me and said, "You know, you're a pretty smart guy, but I think you need to change your image so that other people can get past how you look." I thought about it for a while, and then decided to give it a try. As soon as I went from jeans to slacks, my connect rate tripled.

Now, many of you who grew up in the '60s are screaming at me for compromising my ideals. Here's how I look at it: jeans were compromising my wallet.

I actually liked my new look. And I have spent the last twenty years continuing to develop it. Some of what I wear is risky, but I'm willing to take the risk in order to maintain my style.

If I ask you if you have a style, what would your answer be? When you look at yourself in the mirror in the morning, what do you see? Have you ever asked anyone what you look like? What do others think when they see you?

Or maybe a better question is: What can you upgrade so that others might think something better than they are thinking now? I think you can gather from the last few paragraphs that style has a lot to do with connecting. If I simply say, "Look professional," that doesn't mean anything. I was in a big bank yesterday and all the people in the hallways looked the same. They looked professional. None of them had what I would consider a discernable style.

Style adds to attractiveness. And the wrong style can make you unattractive or unconnectable. Ok, not unconnectable, but certainly less-connectable. Wearing brown shoes with a tuxedo doesn't just look bad, it sounds bad.

I think I've said enough about clothing. I don't want to dwell on it other than to say it's an important part of your connectivity. The easy answer is: Buy more clothes, more often. The harder answer is: As you buy them, make sure they fit your style and the image you seek to project. Even if you're trying for a conservative look, you can still look sharp, and believe me, people will notice either way.

The first class factor

Everyone wants to fly first class. Everyone wants to travel first class. If given a choice, everyone would take what they consider to be the best. Same in making connections.

Your ability to look first class, act first class, talk first class, and be known as first class are the key indicators that your connection will be successful. Having a first-class reputation is a report card that everything else about you is first class.

Wouldn't it be nice if people talked about you behind your back, and began the conversation by saying what a first-class person you are?

Tough questions:

WHAT ARE YOU KNOWN FOR?

WHAT ARE YOU KNOWN AS?

WHAT IS YOUR FOUR-PART REPUTATION?

1. What is your reputation with your company and customers?

2. What is your reputation with your industry?

3. What is your reputation with your community?

4. What is your reputation with your friends and family?

Until those questions are answered, and those elements are firmly established, there's little sense in starting to enter the world of connections. Before you can work on others, you have to work on yourself. You have to become connection-worthy.

PERSONAL CONFESSION: I may not always be known as first class. But I am always known as a world-class expert, or the world-class expert at what I do. I strive to be first class in the way I carry myself and in my style. But I'm not always able to manifest that. I don't believe that first class is something that's constant unless you are constantly striving for it. I do know that all the elements of connecting, and all the principles of connecting that I've listed, are ones that I live and work on daily.

There's a big difference between having a reputation, and worrying about what others think of you. I strive for a great reputation, but I'm not looking to hang myself if someone doesn't think I'm first class. I'll settle for a simple majority, as would anyone striving to be president of the United States the day after the election.

I have discovered that reputation is also built by providing and performing random acts of kindness. Not only does this build reputation, but you also feel great when you perform the deed. It can be as simple as helping an old lady into an airplane, or anonymously buying someone who is hungry a Thanksgiving meal.

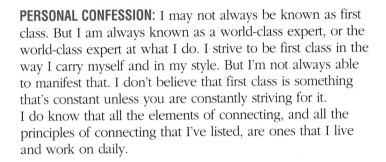

GOAL: When someone talks about you behind your back, you want them to refer to you as **FIRST CLASS**.

The secret and power of "give value first"

Throughout this book, the word **VALUE**, and the value process, have been the dominant theme. It's not just a matter of you connecting with others, it's a matter of others *wanting* to connect with you -- or *desiring* to connect with you.

Just as you expect value from them, just as you want something from them, they too want something from you.

The thread of value runs throughout this book, just as the thread of "Be Yourself" runs through Dale Carnegie's *How to Win Friends and Influence People.* Just as "A definite major aim" runs through Napoleon Hill's *Think and Grow Rich.* It's there one hundred times, so that eventually you will not only get it, but you will act on it. And act in a way that *The Little Black Book of Connections* will provide a pathway to rich relationships.

My theme of *give value first*, actually my mantra of *give value first*, manifests itself in several ways: I give value first with my column, I give value first with *Sales Caffeine*, I give value first with my Web site, and I provide sales information to millions of people weekly so that they can make more sales.

By giving value first, I have created a base of connections, and a basis for wealth. And so can you, if you're willing to give it away before you get it.

UNIVERSAL TRUTH
OF CONNECTING

If you make yourself valuable, and memorable, others will want to make you part of their network.

-- Jeffrey Gitomer

The lifelong connection process

The lifelong connection process has two meanings. Number one is the never-ending search (the lifelong search) for attracting and making new connections. Number two is the process and the dedication to keeping your connections for a lifetime.

Making connections for a lifetime.

Keeping connections for a lifetime.

Once you decide that you're willing to go through the hard work and the self-discipline of both making connections and creating connection awareness, then at once you will realize that there's no time limit attached to it. You're not about to try your hardest for a week, or even a month or a year, and then say to yourself, "Okay, I have enough now, I can stop."

Nor are you about to look at your connection base and say, "I have enough information from them. I can stop connecting with them now. I can stop communicating with them."

Once you start the connection process, you cannot stop. That's the good news. The better news is that your database, or should I say, your asset base, will continue to build in strength and value. As you continue to grow your network, as you continue to grow your connections, so will you continue to grow in success. But the best news is: If you follow my formula of providing value first, your connections will continue to provide endless value back to you.

I've been working at giving value first and the connection process for more than 20 years. The results have been staggering. The results have been beyond my expectations. Actually, the results have been beyond belief. That's part of the compelling reason for writing this book.

I'm not telling you what "to" do, rather I'm sharing with you what I have done, exactly how I did it, and several easy paths for you to do it.

I can't do any more than that. The rest is up to you. My e-mail address is my name, jeffrey@gitomer.com. Connect with me, and let me know how you're doing.

The Journey.

I've heard the saying: "There's only two big decisions in life, where you're going, and who you're going to take with you."

I know where I am going.
I know who I am taking.
I hope you do, too.

JEFFREY GITOMER
Chief Executive Salesman

AUTHOR. Jeffrey is the author of *The New York Times* best seller *The Sales Bible, Customer Satisfaction Is Worthless -- Customer Loyalty Is Priceless, The Patterson Principles of Selling, The Little Red Book of Selling,* and his latest book *The Little Red Book of Sales Answers.*

OVER 100 PRESENTATIONS A YEAR. Jeffrey gives seminars, runs annual sales meetings, and conducts training programs on selling and customer loyalty. He has presented an average of 120 seminars a year for the past ten years.

BIG CORPORATE CUSTOMERS. Jeffrey's customers include Coca-Cola, D.R. Horton, Caterpillar, BMW, BNC Mortgage, Cingular Wireless, MacGregor Golf, Ferguson Enterprises, Kimpton Hotels, Hilton, Enterprise Rent-A-Car, AmeriPride, NCR, Stewart Title, Comcast Cable, Time Warner Cable, Liberty Mutual Insurance, Principal Financial Group, Wells Fargo Bank, Baptist Health Care, BlueCross BlueShield, Carlsberg Beer, Wausau Insurance, Northwestern Mutual, MetLife, Sports Authority, GlaxoSmithKline, AC Neilsen, IBM, The New York Post, and hundreds of others.

IN FRONT OF MILLIONS OF READERS EVERY WEEK.
Jeffrey's syndicated column, *Sales Moves*, appears in more than ninety-five business newspapers worldwide, and is read by more than four million people every week.

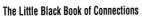

SELLING POWER LIVE. Jeffrey is the host and commentator of *Selling Power Live*, a monthly, subscription-based sales resource bringing together the insights of the world's foremost authorities on selling and personal development.

ON THE INTERNET. Jeffrey's three WOW! Web sites www.gitomer.com, www.trainone.com, and www.knowsuccess.com, get as many as 25,000 hits a day from readers and seminar attendees. His state-of-the-art Web presence and e-commerce ability has set the standard among peers, and has won huge praise and acceptance from customers.

UP YOUR SALES ONLINE SALES TRAINING. Online sales training lessons are available at www.trainone.com. The content is pure Jeffrey -- fun, pragmatic, real-world, and immediately implementable. TrainOne's innovation is leading the way in the field of customized e-learning.

SALES CAFFEINE. Jeffrey's weekly e-zine, *Sales Caffeine*, is a sales wake-up call delivered every Tuesday morning to more than 130,000 subscribers, free of charge. This allows him to communicate valuable sales information, strategies, and answers to sales professionals on a timely basis.

SALES ASSESSMENT ONLINE. The world's first customized sales assessment, renamed a "successment," will not only judge your selling skill level in twelve critical areas of sales knowledge, it will give you a diagnostic report that includes fifty mini sales lessons. This amazing sales tool will rate your sales abilities and explain your customized opportunities for sales knowledge growth. The program is aptly named KnowSuccess because *you can't know success until you know yourself.*

AWARD FOR PRESENTATION EXCELLENCE. In 1997, Jeffrey was awarded the designation of Certified Speaking Professional (CSP) by the National Speakers Association. The CSP award has been given less than 500 times in the past twenty-five years and is the association's highest earned award.

Buy Gitomer, Inc.

310 Arlington Avenue Loft 329, Charlotte, North Carolina, 28203
704-333-1112
www.gitomer.com   jeffrey@gitomer.com

Another Baby

Cracking open a box of "fresh-from-the-printer" books for the first time is an emotional experience that must be experienced rather than talked about.

As a writer, I play an important role in the process of creating a book, but without others, the book you hold in your hands would not be possible.

When I sat with **RAY BARD** in a little Mexican restaurant in Austin three years ago, and he shared his vision of *The Little Red Book of Selling* and other books in a series, it sounded wonderful. But the reality of it is better than the fantasy. And I forever have Ray Bard to thank -- not only for his creative concept, but also for his wisdom, and his integrity -- a rare quality in the publishing world.

When the manuscript is raw, several people play a major role in converting it to the final book product:

JESSICA MCDOUGALL and **RACHEL RUSSOTTO** are not just first class editors, they know my body of work, and they know my voice. In the editing process, it's an imperative to maintain a continuity of style and expression. These women are the masters. Not just from their pens -- but from their hearts. Although Rachel resigned for personal reasons before the project was completed, I appreciate her work and wish her the best. Jessica and I finished the book as the waves pounded against the rocks in Coos Bay, Oregon -- one of the nicest, and most peaceful, places I have ever had the pleasure to visit.

The cover design has gone through one hundred gyrations -- all of which my brother **JOSH GITOMER** has created with love, dedication, more than fifty years of understanding me, and with a response that rivals the speed of summer lightning. Josh's design work also dots some of the inside pages. Considering he's only had a computer in his hands for three years, his graphic prowess transferred from the paste-up board to Photoshop and has been nothing short of remarkable. As grateful as I am for his talent, it pales by comparison to the gratefulness I have for our reunion.

Every page in this book, and every page in my previous four books, have been designed, and energized, with the graphic grace of **GREG RUSSELL**. His understanding of what makes type and layout work has added a dimension to this book that is obvious as you flip through the pages. Books become readable with a combination of words and graphic design. I'm grateful for Greg Russell's excellence in word design.

And if I am going to say thank you and be grateful to people who helped make this book a reality, I would be remiss not to include every connection that I have made from childhood through "immature" adulthood. It's from these connections that I have learned the lessons that I am able to transfer to you. I am not just grateful for my experiences, I am grateful for the friendships, the relationships, the mentorships, and the love I have received.

**Until the next little book appears,
I am Jeffrey Gitomer.
Father, grandfather, friend,
writer, speaker, and lover of life.**

Bibliography

Google

Other titles by Jeffrey Gitomer

THE LITTLE RED BOOK OF SALES ANSWERS
(Pearson Prentice-Hall, 2006)

THE LITTLE RED BOOK OF SELLING
(Bard Press, 2004)

CUSTOMER SATISFACTION IS WORTHLESS, CUSTOMER LOYALTY IS PRICELESS
(Bard Press, 1998)

THE SALES BIBLE
(John Wiley and Sons, 2003)

THE PATTERSON PRINCIPLES OF SELLING
(Lito Press, 2006)

IT'S A LOVELY DIAMOND,
BUT I TOLD YOU TO ENGAGE THE CLIENT.
I DIDN'T TELL YOU TO GET ENGAGED
TO THE CLIENT.

What was
I thinking?

GLASBERGEN